# ADVANCE PRAISE FOR
# *PERFORMANCE-FOCUSED*
# *SMILE SHEETS*

Only a few people combine the rigor of a researcher and the usability of a how-to writer. Will Thalheimer is the best among them. He has done it again in his *Performance-Focused Smile Sheets.* Will has undertaken an audacious project. This book is the beginning of a radical revolution for professionalizing our field. Sign me up.

**Sivasailam Thiagarajan, PhD**
**Principal and "Mad Scientist"at The Thiagi Group**

In a 160-plus billion dollar training industry, debunking and reconstructing traditional smile sheets is way overdue. Kudos to Will Thalheimer for leading the way!

**Ruth Colvin Clark**
**Clark Training & Consulting**

Will Thalheimer attacks one of the most intractable misconceptions in our field, and does so with authority and humor. His straight-shooter approach to improving smile sheets is a wake-up call for the field. Thalheimer's prescription is easily understandable and makes perfect sense. And, any book that equates learning measurement to pure sex has to be a must read!

**Marc J. Rosenberg, PhD**
**Marc Rosenberg and Associates**

What we need in Learning and Development is nothing short of a revolution in the way we evaluate training. The current approach—which in most companies is limited to end-of-class smile sheets—needs to be thrown out. In *Performance-Focused Smile Sheets*, Dr. Will Thalheimer presents revolutionary ideas, as well as practical guidelines and examples for transforming a useless exercise into one of real value and impact. Read this book and you will want to join Will on the front lines of change.

**Roy Pollock, DVM, PhD**
**Chief Learning Officer, 6Ds® Company**
**co-author of *Six Disciplines of Breakthrough Learning***

Will Thalheimer, one of our most reputable translators of research into practice, has written his first book, a readable treatise on that scourge of learning, smile sheets. This insightful (and inciteful) work aptly skewers current approaches and provides a healthy alternative that both helps us now and educates us to do better going forward. A valuable contribution indeed!

**Dr. Clark Quinn**
**Executive Director of Quinnovation**
**author of *Revolutionize Learning & Development***

In our field there can be a lot of hand-waving—general advice without clear application guidelines. Will's book is exactly the opposite. He gives you the deep-dive on level 1 training evaluations, including both the how and the why. This is evidence-based practice at the master level.

**Julie Dirksen**
**Author of *Design For How People Learn***

It's about time that someone took the ubiquitous but mostly useless end-of-session training feedback questionnaire to task. Will Thalheimer does a great job of telling us why the current practice doesn't work and replaces it with thoughtful and sensible advice for feedback tools that will provide valid and actionable data.

**Robert O. Brinkerhoff**
**Professor Emeritus, Western Michigan University**
**& Director, Brinkerhoff Evaluation Institute**

With this book, Will Thalheimer provides an important contribution, particularly in showing how to ensure that learner feedback provides a true gauge of on-the-job success. The book is research-based, comprehensive, and based on real-world experiences. If you're spending time and money in using smile sheets, this book will show you how to make them valuable, useful, and relevant to your organization's success.

**Jack J. Phillips**
**Chairman, ROI Institute**

Freakin' revolutionary or business smart? Will Thalheimer's position is that smile sheets are a waste unless they're designed to predict a change in job behavior—an idea that's refreshing, worthwhile, and, as the book demonstrates, actionable too! I encourage you to read *Performance-Focused Smile Sheets* and reflect on how you might improve the feedback your organization captures from its learners.

**Judith Hale, PhD, CPT, ID (SEL, ILT, JA+)**
**Co-founder Institute for Performance Improvement**

Will Thalheimer's work is grounded in research, honed through experience, and organized to provide a practical perspective for application. In *Performance–Focused Smile Sheets*, Will dissects the current failure of learner-feedback instruments and provides an alternative perspective on what will work; as well as arguments you can use to change organizational cultures that remain wedded to these inaccurate metrics.

**William Coscarelli**
**Professor *Emeritus*,**
**Southern Illinois University**

Will Thalheimer, PhD, is one of the definitive myth busters in our field, and he does it with great precision but also humor. It's good that he's explaining the things we need to know about smile sheets, because there are just too many fairytales. We must be held to a higher standard.

**Patti Shank, PhD**
**Author and Learning Analyst**
**PattiShank.com**

It is hard to do, but Will Thalheimer has found a way to make the measurement of learning sexy and exciting in his book *Performance-Focused Smile Sheets*. You'll find yourself turning the pages and laughing along the way (usually at your own past mistakes, which you won't make again after reading this book).

**Ryan Watkins**
**George Washington University**

Finally, a book that acknowledges and addresses the dirty and widespread problem with smile sheets, which typically tell us nothing useful and focus our attention on the wrong things. Will Thalheimer's book provides useful guidance for using this tool correctly, in ways that improve learning and its transfer to the workplace in ways that produce valued performance. Anyone involved in workplace learning and performance will find this book valuable.

**Steven W. Villachica, PhD**
**Associate Professor**
**Boise State University**

If you are responsible for evaluating training, stop right now and read *Performance-Focused Smile Sheets*. The insights and ideas will change forever how you create evaluations. Quite simply, the BEST book on smile sheet creation and utilization, period!

**Karl M. Kapp**
**Professor of Instructional Technology**
**Bloomsburg University**

What I like most about Thalheimer's book on Performance-Focused Smile Sheets is that it puts the focus where it belongs, predicting subsequent performance on the job—the ultimate measure of learning in an enterprise context. An excellent resource for all Learning Professionals!

**Guy W. Wallace**
**President, EPPIC Inc.**

Thalheimer has replaced the smile sheet beauty pageant with an approach that delivers concretely actionable design insights, reinforces learning, and educates learners and their sponsors about what really matters in learning. He's turned the smile sheet into a tool capable of delivering substantial performance impact for both individuals and businesses.

**Adam Neaman, PhD**
**former Manager of Technology-Enabled**
**Learning Design, Mckinsey & Co.**

Armed with a lot of heart and incredible insights, this book oozes with mind-blowing, radical, myth-busting, research-proven takeaways from the master of learning research, Will Thalheimer. This is a must read, and a must apply, for anyone involved in education, learning, and evaluation; from conferences to workshops to online education.

**Jeff Hurt, EVP, Education & Engagement,**
**Velvet Chainsaw Consulting**

# PERFORMANCE-FOCUSED SMILE SHEETS

# PERFORMANCE-FOCUSED SMILE SHEETS

## A Radical Rethinking of a Dangerous Art Form

# Will Thalheimer, PhD

Work-Learning Press

ISBN-13: 978-1-941577-00-4
LCCN: 2015918613

Distributed by Itasca Books

Book Design by Sophie Chi

*Printed in the United States of America*

# DEDICATION

For many, many years, I've had the following dedication written down, waiting for my first book to be published. I want to use this chance to honor those who have given me the most.

- To my mom and dad, Kay and Bill, who somehow—in a way that I regret I'll never fully understand—prepared the soil for my growth and learning.
- To my wife, Dorothy, who has allowed me my mission—through the struggle, despair, and joys of the journey.
- To my daughter, Alena, whose thirteen-year-old soul and luminous eyes remind me daily that learning is at the heart of our humanity.

# Contents

# ACKNOWLEDGMENTS

BOOKS DON'T GET WRITTEN or published by themselves. I am grateful to my wife, Dorothy, and my daughter, Alena, who have allowed me time to write and think. I am indebted to thousands of research scientists, journal editors and publishers, libraries, and database creators for enabling me to learn from the research. I am thankful to my clients who have made it possible over the past seventeen years for me to make a living and continue my work.

Specific thanks go to Doug Holt and Russ Spaulding for enabling me to share some of the underlying concepts of the Performance-Focused Smile Sheet before they were fully formed. Thanks to all the folks who gave me advice on book publishing, including Mark Klein, Chad Udell, Clark Quinn, Julie Dirksen, Michael Allen, Ruth Clark, Allison Rossett, Roy Pollock, and various members of the Maine Writers and Publishers Alliance.

Thanks to Kate Ankofski and Katherine Pickett for their incredibly helpful editing. I had no idea that so many improvements could be made.

Special thanks go to Jack Phillips, Rob Brinkerhoff, Bill Coscarelli, Clark Quinn, Adam Neaman, and Julie Dirksen, for giving me in-depth feedback on the initial draft of this book—helping me improve it immeasurably.

# PREFACE

I'VE BEEN DOING LEARNING SINCE I reached adulthood. I taught emotionally disturbed kids how to act as Boy Scouts. I taught a young woman whose body and mind had been devastated by meningitis—who had almost no control over her arms—how to reach to grab a spoon. It took six weeks. I got into an MBA program so that I could find a job, but found that instructional-design courses were much more rewarding. I got work as an instructional designer and designed an "MBA in a box." I built simulations to teach leadership and management skills. I parlayed this into an opportunity to build two simulations to teach at-risk high-school students in Brooklyn on how to run a business. I taught teachers-in-training about educational psychology. They taught me that I knew nothing about schools. I taught leadership courses and change-management courses to managers in Fortune 500 companies. I even taught business strategy a few times with learners polite enough not to laugh at my lack of depth. For seventeen years, I've been teaching instructional designers, trainers, and elearning developers about the research on learning.

I was lucky. When I started Work-Learning Research in 1998 I had very few responsibilities. No family to help support. No mortgage to pay. I could earn enough money to support myself by selling my skills as a leadership trainer. Most of my time was spent wonderfully lost in the research on learning, memory, and instruction. My aim was to uncover a short list of fundamental learning factors in an otherwise chaotic sea of experimental results. The task was huge—too big for me to succeed in the short term. But swimming in the vast depths of the research, I began to understand human learning at a deeper level than I could have previously contemplated. I also learned how daunting the task, how impossible! Over the years, I've kept my research going a good portion of the time. It's an important task—bridging the gap between research and practice—but unfortunately, it's one that the world doesn't easily support in the learning field. Still, I'm grateful that I've had the time.

I took this path because I believed strongly—and still believe—that learning is a noble cause. It is learning that has enabled human civilization and growth. It is learning that enables individuals to excel and thrive. It is learning that holds the promise of the future.

If learning is so important and our task is such a noble one, don't we, as learning professionals, have an almost sacred responsibility to do our jobs well?

The way I see it, there are two main lynchpins to our performance. First, scientific research must guide our starting assumptions. Second, we must use good learning measurement to get valid feedback so that we can refine our understandings, improve our learning designs, and live up to our promise—so that we can maximize the benefits of learning.

This book focuses on the second imperative. It examines the popular yet downtrodden smile sheet and attempts to elevate it to full effectiveness. While smile sheets should never be the only way we get feedback on learning, by improving them, we can get significantly better information about how we're doing. With better information, we can create virtuous cycles of continuous improvement. We can build more effective learning interventions and meet our obligations as learning professionals.

# INTRODUCTION

FOR SEVENTEEN YEARS I'VE BEEN exhaustively reviewing research on how people learn, reading an average of over two hundred articles every year from scientific refereed journals. Doing the research has enabled me to build a consulting practice where I can provide workplace learning professionals with research-inspired insights. It has also compelled me—and I really can't help myself—to think about the state of the learning profession. This is not always a happy endeavor.

One thing I noticed a few years ago was that we as workplace-learning professionals often work in darkness. We get most of our feedback from smile sheets—also known as happy sheets, postcourse evaluations, student-response forms, training-reaction surveys, and so on. We also get feedback from knowledge tests. Unfortunately, both smile sheets and knowledge tests are often flawed in their execution, providing dangerously misleading information. Yet, without valid feedback, it is impossible for us to know how successful we've been in our learning designs. I'm writing this book to help you get better feedback and to help your organization produce more effective learning initiatives. I'm focusing here on smile sheets because they are so central to our work in today's workplace-learning industry.

We, as workplace learning-and-performance professionals, often see smile sheets as a small thing—when they are in fact a huge, dark, and demonic colossus. More than any other tool in the training-and-development industry, smile sheets control what we do. They are a self-inflicted form of mind control, warping our thoughts from learning's essential realities. Smile sheets—as now designed—do not just tell us nothing. They tell us worse than nothing. They focus our worries toward the wrong things. They make us think our learning interventions are more effective than they are. More than any other practice in our field, they have done the most damage.

In brief, here are the problems with traditional smile sheets:

1. They are not correlated with learning results.

2. They don't tell us whether our learning interventions are good or bad.

3. They misinform us about what improvements should be made.

4. They don't enable meaningful feedback loops.

5. They don't support smile-sheet decision making.

6. They don't help stakeholders understand smile-sheet results.

7. They provide misleading information.

8. They hurt our organizations by not enabling cycles of continuous improvement.

9. They create a culture of dishonest deliberation.

This book aims to stop the bleeding.

Some of you may not be familiar with the term "smile sheet." Others may wonder why I am appropriating a word that has a derogatory meaning. Those of you who are mindful of future trends may be wondering why I'm using a term that connotes paper-and-pencil responding when more and more smile sheets are being delivered electronically.

Smile sheets are also known as happy sheets, student-response forms, trainee reaction surveys, and so forth. I've decided to use the term "smile sheet" because it is the most commonly used term, it has a long history of use, and it conjures elemental conceptions that need a massive dose of reform.

My hope for this book is simple: to help you get significantly better insight into the factors that drive your learning results—so that you can improve your current learning practices. By reading this book, you will learn how to create a Performance-Focused Smile Sheet. You will look at your current smile sheets in a whole new light—as if seeing them for the first time. With newfound wisdom, you'll know how to radically improve your smile sheets, providing you and your stakeholders with a unique and enlightening vision of your learning outcomes! The smile sheets you will build will be inspired by the learning research, will help your learners produce more useful information, and will focus not just on the learning event but also on the situations and factors that enable the learning to culminate in successful real-world accomplishments.

# WHY THIS BOOK IS WORTH YOUR TIME

1. The methods presented in this book will help you to create smile sheets that will provide you and your stakeholders with truly valuable data and information—of the kind that will enable you to create virtuous cycles of continuous improvement, and thus, significantly better learning outcomes for your learners and your organization.

2. This book is research-based. It draws its recommendations from the world's best learning research, from the preeminent refereed scientific journals on learning, memory, and instruction.

3. This book is comprehensive. It offers a complete system for developing smile sheets.

4. This book is born of real-world experience. It acknowledges that research alone is not worth anything without practical wisdom.

5. This book is designed to help you learn. It will support your learning as much as the book format allows.

6. This book is a "call to arms." It takes an honest look at the training-and-development field and our poor measurement practices. It celebrates sound ideas. It fumes angrily at bad practices.

7. This book follows the aphorism often attributed to Albert Einstein, "Everything should be made as simple as possible, but no simpler."[1] It simplifies complex realities into workable recommendations.

---

[1] Ironically, these words were probably not actually stated by Einstein, but are rather a simplification of the sentence, "It can scarcely be denied that the supreme goal of all theory is to make the irreducible basic elements as simple and as few as possible without having to surrender the adequate representation of a single datum of experience," as described on http://en.wikiquote.org/wiki/Albert_Einstein and in more detail at http://quoteinvestigator.com/2011/05/13/einstein-simple/#more-2363.

# WHO WILL FIND VALUE
## IN THIS BOOK

THIS BOOK WILL BENEFIT workplace-learning professionals who want to improve the design and delivery of their learning interventions.

**Learning measurement professionals**—practitioners responsible for smile sheets, assessments of learning and performance, and learning-based organizational results.

**Creators of learning interventions**—instructional designers, trainers, elearning developers, teachers, professors, and other educators.

**Managers of learning**—chief learning officers, learning executives, training managers, conference-education professionals, and instructional-development managers.

**Graduate students and faculty**—in learning measurement, assessment, instructional design, instructional technology, elearning, performance improvement, and adult learning.

*Performance-Based Smile Sheets* is ideal for experienced practitioners who want to (1) energize their current practices with research-based recommendations, (2) challenge themselves with unique and provocative perspectives, and (3) prepare for the future of the learning-design field.

# CHAPTER 1

## WHAT ARE SMILE SHEETS FOR?

IMAGINE YOURSELF AS THE chief learning officer of a global corporation. You've been with the company seven years, working your way up, reveling in the success of the workplace learning-and-performance function. Suddenly, your CEO retires and a new CEO is hired. In her late thirties, Julie Sendirk is known as an innovator and a straight shooter. After a month or so and several meetings, Sendirk calls you into her office and asks you to help her understand the annual report your department created.

Julie:      "Hey, welcome! Here's what I'm interested in, and I need your help. In general, I want to understand how you learning folks operate. Today, I want to drill down on the smile-sheet results from the past year. If I read this report right, it says that overall, our training courses have an average rating of about 4.1? Is that accurate?"

You:       "Yes, and 82% of our courses are rated at 4.5 or better. We're very proud of our results. We've worked hard to improve our ratings over the last three years."

Julie:      "But what does a 4.1 actually mean?"

You:       "It means that we're doing well, that the training is well received. It's a 4.1 on a 1-to-5 scale, so we can't get much higher."

Julie:        "But what does the 4.1 actually mean?"

You:          [controlling the urge to talk louder] "Well, at the end of every training class, we give learners a set of questions about their perceptions of the training."

Julie:        "And each question has a 1–5 scale?"

You:          "No, actually. Each question is really a statement, and the learners select one of five answer choices, from 'strongly disagree,' which gets a 1, to 'strongly agree,' which gets a 5."

Julie:        "So a 4.1 means that most people 'agree,' and if they don't select 'agree,' they likely selected 'strongly agree,' and if not, then they've probably chosen 'neither agree nor disagree?'"

You:          "Yes, that's exactly right. Pretty simple, really."

Julie:        "Hmm. But what does a 4.1 mean? It certainly can't mean that our employees tend to be agreeable?"

You:          "Well, no. . . ."

Julie:        [cutting you off] "So the 4.1 is an average of the dozen or so questions you ask?"

You:          "Well, no, in the annual report we just share the results of one question, our main question."

Julie:        [now looking skeptical] "So you collect more than 10 times the data than that which you share with senior management?"

You:          [starting to sweat] "Well, in our experience—and let me apologize for saying this—most senior managers just want the overall scores."

Julie:        "So what is this overarching question you ask, your main question as you call it—the one that answers the question I asked earlier, 'What does 4.1 mean?'"

You: "We ask the learners to rate the overall value of the course. The question statement reads, 'This training provided valuable job-relevant information that supports on-the-job performance.'"

Julie: "Hmm. And what evidence do you have that the learners are good at evaluating the value of training? What evidence do you have that your main question is associated with actual on-the-job performance?"

You: "It's a training-industry standard."

Julie: "And this standard is based on trusted scientific research?"

You: "Well, I haven't actually seen the research, but I'm sure the learning-measurement experts rely on the best research."

Julie: "Have we done any studies to show that this one question is valid with our learners and the content areas in our organization? So for example, if we get high scores on this question, do we know whether our employees are more likely to be successful on the job than if they've been in a course that gets a low rating?"

You: "We've seen that this question is correlated to our other smile-sheet questions, so we're pretty confident."

Julie: "But that's not what I'm asking. Of course the questions are correlated, probably because people just circle the same numbers down the smile sheet. What I want to know is whether our smile-sheet results—the one's you show management every year—are related to on-the-job performance. Do we know that?"

You: "They should be." [Here you go into a long discussion of the Kirkpatrick four-level model of training evaluation.]

Julie:      "Has this model been tested? Does it show that smile sheets are correlated with learning results? And even if it has been tested generally, how do we know our smile sheets are correlated with our learning results?"

You:        "The Kirkpatrick model has been around since the 1960s."

Julie:      [acting highly skeptical] "All right! Thank you! Here's what I want. I want a way to measure how effective our training courses are in helping our employees understand the concepts and skills they're being taught. I also want to know whether our employees are able to remember the concepts and skills and whether they're successful in applying them to their jobs."

You:        "We can do that, but it costs more money to measure learning and application. We occasionally do some of this kind of measurement, but most previous senior leaders didn't want to pay for it."

Julie:      "Make a business case, and I'll definitely pay for it. I don't know how you guys can operate in the dark, without getting any feedback on how you're really doing. But what about these smile sheets? Can't you improve them to at least give you some idea of how effective the training has been?"

Okay, this is Will again. Let me apologize for putting you into the role of an almost-clueless CLO. Just like I tell my daughter, you'll thank me for it later. SMILE. The truth is that Julie, our savvy new CEO, asked some damn good questions—questions we in the training-and-development field don't always ask ourselves. I'm starting the book with this example to show how our traditional approach to smile sheets may have a few chinks in its armor—and also to get your blood flowing a bit. We'll go into more depth about the issues this case presents, but first, let me cover some basics to make sure we're on the same page.

## What Is a Smile Sheet?

A smile sheet is a set of questions provided to learners after training—or after a portion of training—asking for learners' perceptions of the value of the training. Smile sheets are also known as happy sheets, student-response forms, trainee reaction surveys, and so forth. In fact, the terms "smile sheet" and "happy sheet" are often considered to have a derogatory connotation. The feeling among many practitioners is that smile sheets have minimal value or provide misleading results. Despite these concerns, smile sheets are the most popular way to get evaluative feedback about the success of workplace training—and the same is true in higher education.

Smile sheets are often placed within a framework of other learning-measurement methods. By far the most popular of these frameworks is the Kirkpatrick four-level model of learning evaluation. The Kirkpatrick Model's four levels are:

1. Learner Reaction

2. Learning Results

3. On-the-job Behavioral Results

4. Organizational Results

Learners' reactions are almost always measured through smile sheets. Learning can be measured in many ways, including tests, skill demonstrations, scenario-based questions, and more. On-the-job behavioral results are often measured with self-report data, but can be measured through observations of actual performance, ratings from others, and objective performance measures such as time-of-task completion. Organizational results are usually measured with organizational data that is already collected by the organization, such as sales revenues, costs, and customer satisfaction. While the Kirkpatrick Model is widely used, it is also widely criticized for its shortcomings. We will touch on these shortcomings in Chapter 2. For now, it's critical to understand that for many people, the Kirkpatrick Model signifies that smile sheets are related to the other four levels.

Smile sheets can be utilized for many reasons.[2] Here's a short list, which I've modified slightly from learning-measurement expert Rob Brinkerhoff:

1. Red-flagging training programs that are not sufficiently effective.

2. Gathering ideas for ongoing updates and revision of a learning program.

3. Judging strengths and weaknesses of a pilot program to enable revision.

4. Providing instructors with feedback to aid their development.

5. Helping learners reflect on and reinforce what they learned.

6. Helping learners determine what (if anything) they plan to do with their learning.

7. Capturing learner satisfaction data to understand—and make decisions that relate to—the reputation of the training and/or the instructors.

8. Upholding the spirit of common courtesy by giving learners a chance for feedback.

9. Enabling learner frustrations to be vented—to limit damage from negative back-channel communications.

Most traditional smile sheets are pretty good at numbers 7, 8, and 9 above—getting learner satisfaction data, providing a feedback mechanism out of common courtesy, and enabling learners to vent their frustrations. I'm on my high horse in this book to help us all develop better feedback loops so that we can create virtuous cycles of continuous improvement. Within the list above, this book is aimed at helping us do much better on numbers 1 through 4, which I'll repeat here to emphasize them:

---

2    Special thanks to Rob Brinkerhoff for reminding me of this truth and for providing me with a list of reasons that I am sharing with you now in a somewhat modified form.

1.  Red-flagging training programs that are not sufficiently effective.

2.  Gathering ideas for ongoing updates and revision of a learning program.

3.  Judging strengths and weaknesses of a pilot program to enable revision.

4.  Providing instructors with feedback to aid their development.

The bottom line for me is that we need to get good feedback so that we can improve what we're doing.

That's my belief, but you and your organization are going to have to determine for yourselves what you want to get out of your smile sheets. Indeed, one key to successful evaluation is to first figure out why you're doing what you're doing. I recommend that you get your team together to reflect on the above nine-item list and see what you want to accomplish with your smile sheets. Only then should you start your smile-sheet design work.

## Learning Measurement is Pure Sex!

I received a call recently asking me to speak at an industry meeting. The caller said she loved my work and anything I wanted to talk about would be great. Because of all the love and goodwill I was hearing, I brimmed with warm fuzzies as I recited half a dozen topics I could speak on. When we got to the topic of "Performance-Focused Smile Sheets" I practically oozed with elation. I talked about their importance and how recent audiences—even of learning executives—trembled in delight when they learned that traditional smile sheets could actually be dangerous. The person I was speaking with got fired up too, but said this: "Learning measurement just isn't sexy enough to draw people to our meeting, so I think we should go with another topic."

What the heck? Learning measurement isn't sexy enough? Let me start this book by saying that learning measurement is pure sex—with titillating foreplay, naked truth, and the dangerous rapture of the potential for new life. Seriously! Learning measurement is one of the most important topics in training and development—especially because most learning measurement is gravely incompetent.

I've been on the warpath of learning measurement for almost a decade. I've written articles on learning-measurement bias. I've done numerous keynote addresses, featured sessions, invited masters presentations, and workshops on learning measurement. I almost always bring up the need for better learning measurement with my consulting clients. Why am I—a research-guzzling learning consultant—so crazy about learning measurement? Because learning measurement gives us feedback! It gives us feedback so that we can improve what we're doing. It is one of the most important things that we do! Without adequate feedback loops, we simply can't know whether we're doing any good at all. We can't know what to improve—or whether to improve. Without getting good feedback we frankly aren't worthy of the title "professionals."

In the diagram that follows, you'll notice the tried-and-true instructional-design process. In it, feedback loops show how the instructional-design process is supposed to work. We are supposed to get routine feedback so we

# The Instructional-Design Process

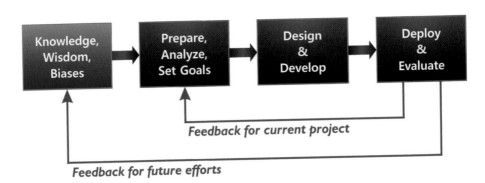

Feedback for current project

Feedback for future efforts

can improve our current efforts and also improve our knowledge and wisdom, while reducing our biases. Rarely does it work as diagrammed.

We tend to measure learning at the end of learning events, which seems sensible, but it doesn't take into account eons of research on human learning and forgetting. When we measure at the end of learning, we are only measuring our learners' *understanding* at that point in time; we are *not* measuring their ability to *remember* after the learning event. Look at the next diagram. You can see that if we measure at the end of the learning event, the learners are at their highest level of memory retrieval. Of course! Everything at the end of training is top-of-mind. Things are easy to recall. When we measure at the end of learning, we are getting biased results. We are getting results that make us—and our learning interventions—look a whole lot better than the truth.

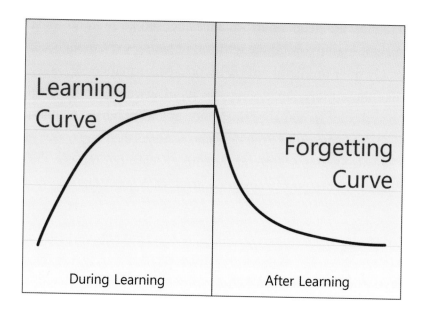

Similarly, when we measure in the learning context, we are also biasing our results. People aren't like computers. We don't just retrieve perfect packets of information from memory; we access a full range of associated memories. When a person is in the same context that they learned in, the stimuli in that context will remind them of what they learned. If the learning context is not the work context, then measuring learning in the learning context will produce more and better memory retrieval than the work context will—again producing biased learning-measurement results.

A third learning-measurement bias entails how we are measuring. As Sharon Shrock and Bill Coscarelli have pointed out in their brilliant book on criterion-referenced test development, the best measure of performance competence is actual performance.[3] If we're teaching someone to drive a

---

3   Shrock & Coscarelli (2007).

forklift, the best way to measure their competence will be to have them drive a forklift—preferably in the same conditions they'll face on the job. If we can't measure real-world performance, we can simulate or have the learners make authentic scenario-based decisions as reasonable proxies for performance. What we don't want to do is to just test learners on their knowledge of simple facts. Unfortunately, because it is a lot easier to measure simple knowledge than it is to measure deeper performance-focused know-how, most learning measurement is biased toward the retrieval of facts—even though such metrics are extremely poor predictors of real-world performance.

Just like these more direct assessments of learning, smile sheets should likewise be relevant to actual performance and as unbiased as possible. But, alas, most smile sheets suffer from the same issues as the three biases mentioned above. They are deployed only at the end of learning, only in the learning context, and only with poorly designed, irrelevant questions.

# Chapter 2

# Your Smile Sheets Suck!

MOST PEOPLE I TALK WITH don't really like smile sheets but see them as a necessary requirement in their organizations—and at least somewhat valuable. I will admit to the same feelings. I spent several years as a leadership trainer, helping managers to become effective leaders. At first I didn't do well on my smile sheets, but over time—partly by taking smile-sheet comments seriously—I got reasonably good as a leadership trainer.

That being said, in this chapter, I'm going to prove to you, as effectively as I can, that your smile sheets suck! My apologies for using such a harsh word. Some of the people I respect most in my life will certainly bristle at the word "*suck*"—but I'm going to break with protocol here because I want to leave no doubt in your mind. Your smile sheets suck![4]

## Research on Smile Sheets

I'll start with the research. Do smile sheets relate to learning results? Are learners' responses on smile sheets related to their ability to understand, remember, or apply what they've learned? Presumably, we are providing smile sheets because we—wise and honorable learning professionals that we are—want to know how effective our learning interventions are in producing benefits. We certainly wouldn't want to waste people's time giving them training that wasn't fully effective, would we?

---

4    Of course, some who read this book will undoubtedly use great smile sheets. If you're one of them, I applaud you and ask your forgiveness for painting with such a broad stroke.

Fortunately, there has been a ton of top-flight scientific research on this very question. In 1997, George Alliger, Scott Tannenbaum, Winston Bennett, Holly Traver, and Allison Shotland gathered together thirty-four scientific studies on the potency of smile sheets and meta-analyzed the results. They found that smile sheets were basically uncorrelated with learning results! To be specific, they were minutely correlated with learning-test results at a correlation of .09. You will remember from your statistics that correlations go from -1 to 1. Correlations between -.30 and .30 are considered weak correlations. Having a correlation of .09 is practically no correlation at all. It would be like correlating the household level of peanut butter use with the household level of television use.

This 1990s meta-analysis should have stopped us from relying so heavily on smile sheets. Yet, somehow we could not help ourselves, and the popularity of smile sheets continued. To put a wooden stake through the heart of this blood-sucking vampire (the traditional smile sheet), another set of researchers did their own meta-analysis more recently. In 2008, Traci Sitzmann, Kenneth Brown, Wendy Casper, Katherine Ely, and Ryan Zimmerman looked at 136 studies and found the exact same thing. Smile-sheet results were correlated with learning results at .09—practically no correlation at all.

These two meta-analyses covering over a hundred studies from the scientific research tell us that smile sheets are not predictive of learning results. Instead of wasting time, money, and energy in using smile sheets, we'd be just as well off if we flipped a coin to determine whether a training course was good or bad. Seriously! The bottom line is that traditional smile sheets are not predictive of important learning outcomes. Indeed, by relying on them we are exhibiting superstitious behavior unbecoming of a true professional.

Neil Rackham—famous for his work doing research on the sales process and discovering that the best salespeople are not those who have the strongest closing technique, but are those who listen the best—tells a cautionary tale about smile-sheet ratings.[5] He was asked by a company what to do with two sales trainers who consistently got the worst smile-sheet ratings. The company wondered whether to fire them, coach them, or punish them in some way.

---

5    Somewhere, many years ago, I heard Neil Rackham tell his story. Later, in 2006, Sarah Boehle wrote a *Training Magazine* article about that story (Boehle, 2006).

Rackham asked the company if he could look more deeply. He decided that he had to look beyond the smile-sheet ratings and look at the after-training success of the learners. What he found was that the learners for the two "failing" sales trainers actually sold the most. They received the worst smile-sheet ratings, but their learners actually learned the most! These black-sheep sales trainers apparently used more rigorous training methods than their peers—and they got the best results; except on the smile sheets.

In Rackham's real-world example, smile sheets did not show a strong positive correlation with performance. They showed exactly the opposite. As the meta-analyses show, the reverse happens too: for some training programs, the highest smile-sheet ratings can be associated with the best learning results. Unfortunately, the thing is that we can't tell when traditional smile sheets will be predictive and when they won't.

Just so you don't think I'm the only one who has pointed out that smile-sheet ratings tell us nothing, let me quote from Richard Clark and Fred Estes's book, *Turning Research Into Results*. They wrote this about smile sheets:

> *People often give very positive ratings to ineffective performance programs. Reaction forms [smile sheets] ask people what they liked the most. What they like, however, is not always what helps them perform better. . . . The reverse can also happen. A successful program can be judged to be ineffective because it asks participants to change something very basic about their beliefs, expectations, and behavior.* (p. 8)

And, because many of us have been raised on the nipple of the Kirkpatrick four-level model of training evaluation and can't imagine that the model and its Level 1 smile-sheet recommendation might be flawed, let me share with you a quote from a recent review article from the top-tier scientific journal *Psychological Science in the Public Interest*:

> *Historically, organizations and training researchers have relied on Kirkpatrick's [four-level] hierarchy as a framework for evaluating training programs. . . . The Kirkpatrick framework has a number of theoretical and practical shortcomings.*

> *[It] is antithetical to nearly 40 years of research on human*
> *learning, leads to a checklist approach to evaluation (e.g., 'we*
> *are measuring Levels 1 and 2, so we need to measure Level*
> *3'), and, by ignoring the actual purpose for evaluation, risks*
> *providing no information of value to stakeholders.* (Salas,
> Tannenbaum, Kraiger, & Smith-Jentsch, 2012, p. 91)

The research I've cited so far is pretty damning of the learning-measurement practices that we in the training-and-development industry employ. It not only reflects appallingly on our field but also shows that what we are doing has to change.

Let me offer one final example of how smile sheets provide inaccurate information—this time from my own work evaluating training programs. I was doing work for an organization that created training materials used by instructors to help learners become entrepreneurs.

Previously—before I'd been called in—the organization had measured success by asking instructors to rate the course. That's all they measured. They had never tested actual learning results. Typically, they found that instructors rated the course at about 4.5 on a 5-point scale—an excellent result. I found similar results. For me, instructors rated the course materials at a 4.5 on a 5-point scale. However, learners rated the course significantly lower, giving the online portion of the course a rating of 3.3 and the classroom portion of the course a 3.8 rating.

Here's the kicker: actual objective measures of the course's impact showed no improvement—pretest to posttest—on realistic scenario-based questions. That is, when they answered scenario-based questions on the posttest linked to similar questions on the pretest, learners showed zero improvement. Indeed, on the posttest they averaged 31% correct on four-item multiple-choice questions that would have been answered with pure guessing at 25% correct! Moreover, the business plans created by the learners as part of the course were some of the worst business plans ever seen by the expert reviewers! Two of the reviewers were so alarmed that they made a special effort to contact me and implore me to let the poor quality be known.

Now imagine if the organization had decided only to use smile-sheet ratings, which you'll remember produced an overall average rating of 3.3 and a classroom-only rating of 3.8. They would have concluded that the course outcomes were average to slightly above average. Or what if the organization had relied only on the results from the instructor version of the smile sheet, which produced a rating of 4.5? They would have been thrilled with an excellent result. But the truth is that the course produced terrible outcomes. It created no improvement on well-designed scenario-based questions and terrible work products—not the stuff of successful training. Again, traditional smile sheets failed to predict important learning outcomes.

Perhaps your smile sheets are different from the hundreds of smile sheets evaluated by the research. Perhaps you've devised smile sheets that go beyond what most learning-measurement books and learning-measurement gurus recommend. But I'm betting that just like most traditional smile sheets, your smile sheets suck!

## Autopsy of the Traditional Smile Sheet

Let me draw on Charles Dickens to imbue my next point with a bit of gravitas.

Today, I declare to the entire world that the traditional smile sheet is dead. It was dead to begin with. There is no doubt whatever about that. Let us register its burial with the clergyman, the clerk, the undertaker, and the chief mourners. Let me sign my name to it. The traditional smile sheet is as dead as a door-nail. This must be distinctly understood, or nothing wonderful can come of the arguments I am going to convey herein (with sincere and loving apologies to Charles Dickens).

Just as Charles Dickens's Scrooge is often seen as a metaphor for institutionalized greed among the most powerful and the possibility that even wayward souls can find redemption if only they are shown the light, the story of the smile sheet in today's workplace learning-and-performance industry can be borne in a similar illumination. Without Dickens's skill, but with conviction, let me raise the ghost of Marley for this good purpose. Let me note, in passing, that powerful mourners will likely attempt to raise the dead corpse of the smile sheet—and perhaps have Marley slain doubly and decisively, chasing off the three specters: truth, effectiveness, and professionalism.

The traditional smile sheet is dead from many fatal blows—not merely one or two. I will highlight them in turn.

But first, let me remind you, dear reader, of one of the most fundamental principles of measurement. There is no perfect measurement instrument! Our efforts in learning measurement should be aimed at producing measurement instruments that are as good as they can be. For our smile sheets, we should aim to increase validity, reliability, and effectiveness. We should aim to improve the decision making of our smile-sheet respondents—increasing their attention, minimizing bias, and focusing on the most relevant aspects of the learning intervention and the learning ecosystem. The results will not reach perfection, but they can produce meaningful results.

## Subjective Inputs

First and foremost, smile sheets are based on subjective inputs of learners—and subjective assessments made by human beings are often flawed. This does not mean that subjective judgments can't have value. They can.[6] But before we look to smile-sheet results as gospel, we must recognize the problems inherent in subjective opinions. Then, we must minimize the deleterious effects of such weaknesses. Finally, when we're looking at smile-sheet results, we must view and reconcile the results in light of the weaknesses inherent in subjective inputs. The ideas in this book will help us minimize the subjectivity penalty, but will not eliminate it.

*"But Dr. Thalheimer, aren't we dishonoring our learners by not trusting their intuitions?"* Nonsense! Certainly we should honor our learners' intuitions, but only after we help surface those intuitions in a way that doesn't bias them. *"But is this really necessary? Aren't learners knowledgeable enough about their own circumstances to respond accurately to our questions?"* No, they are not!

Learners, like all humans, have many accurate perceptions and many inaccurate ones. Moreover, all human beings can be swayed by situational cues toward and away from accuracy and precision. Did you know that if a woman touches your shoulder when you are making a risky decision—whether you're a man or a woman—you will be more willing to take the riskiest option? Did you know that you're more likely to be influenced by a better-looking person than an average-looking person? (Not in writing, fortunately for me.) Did you know that you are more likely to drive slowly if there are trees alongside a road than if there are no trees? We, as human beings, are nudged this way and that

---

6    But we have to be sensitive to when and how subjective inputs have value.

by contextual cues in every situation we face. It's the same for our learners. As we will discuss, the smile sheet context often nudges learners toward bias.

Finally, learners are not always accurate in assessing their own learning. For example, learners are overly optimistic about their ability to remember what they've learned, so they tend to fail to give themselves enough repetitions.[7] Learners fail to utilize retrieval practice to support long-term remembering.[8] Learners don't always overcome their incorrect prior knowledge when reading.[9] Learners often fail to utilize examples in ways that would foster deeper learning.[10] These scientific findings don't mean that learners are always wrong about their own learning, but they do show that learners are often inaccurate.[11] Therefore, if we are counting on learners to give us accurate appraisals of the success of a learning intervention, we are asking more of them than they can deliver. We simply must be skeptical of subjective inputs. We also must do whatever we can to limit the problems inherent in subjective inputs. As you will see below, traditional smile sheets fail in numerous ways to support learners in making unbiased smile-sheet responses.

## Likert-Like Scales Create Poor Smile-Sheet Decision Making

Likert-like scales are ubiquitous on smile sheets—but they are very problematic and should be avoided in most circumstances. I know I'm going completely against most training-industry practices in saying this, but it's the truth. Likert-like scales create poor data on smile sheets!

Likert-like scales provide a statement and ask learners to choose between answer choices. For example:

- Strongly Agree
- Agree

---

7   Zechmeister & Shaughnessy (1980).

8   Karpicke, Butler, & Roediger (2009).

9   Kendeou & van den Broek (2005).

10  Renkl (1997).

11  For two recent reviews that show that learners don't always know best, see Brown, Roediger & McDaniel (2014); Kirschner & van Merriënboer (2013).

- Neither Agree Nor Disagree

- Disagree

- Strongly Disagree

Or, they provide a question and ask learners to choose among answers:

- Extremely satisfied

- Very satisfied

- Somewhat satisfied

- Somewhat dissatisfied

- Very dissatisfied

- Extremely dissatisfied

Likert-like scales are especially problematic because they don't give learners clear distinctions between the answer choices. This creates three issues: (a) it nudges learners away from taking their responses seriously; (b) it creates indecision that can make biased responding more likely, and (c) it produces cognitive fatigue that can lessen the attention learners give to their responses.

One of the most critical things to understand about smile sheets is that learners are making decisions when they answer smile-sheet questions—and such decisions can be swayed by lack of attention and by contextual cues (and by the combination of the two). Therefore, we as learning professionals have to do everything in our power to improve smile-sheet decision making! Likert-like scales harm decision making and so should be avoided as much as possible. It's a lot tougher to decide between "Strongly Agree" and "Agree" than between two more-concrete answer choices. Of course, there may be some circumstances when a Likert-like scale is the perfect methodology, but these situations will be few and far between.

Sharon Shrock and Bill Coscarelli, authors of the classic text, now in its third edition, *Criterion-Referenced Test Development*, offer the following wisdom on using Likert-like descriptive scales:

> *The resulting scale is deficient in that the [response words] are open to many interpretations.* (p. 188)

*"But, Dr. Thalheimer, why do so many surveys and personality diagnostics use Likert-like scales?"* Answer: Because it's easy, it's the tradition, and these tools—unlike smile sheets—can create psychometric advantages by repeating the same concepts in multiple questions and then comparing one category to another category.

In most instances, however, Likert-like scales are ineffective at best. They don't allow learners to make good decisions. A person deciding between "Strongly Agree" and "Agree" will create less precision than a person deciding between two more descriptive statements.

*But, Dr. Thalheimer, don't Likert-like scales have the advantage of placing all our questions on the same continuum—so that we can compare them one to another?* No, they don't. This is a silly fantasy—as if the question stems themselves had no bearing on whether the responses are comparable!

The bottom line is that in most cases we can help our learners make good decisions by avoiding Likert-like scales—and using more descriptive answer choices.

## Smile-Sheet Timing

In a research study I led with the eLearning Guild, we found that 90% of learning measurement occurred at the end of the learning event. Indeed, in the many workshops and conference presentations I have given over the years, this is the standard response of audience members. Most smile sheets are given immediately at the end of learning. Recently, this trend seems to be reversing slightly. With the increase in computer-based smile sheets delivered to the worksite soon after learning, more smile sheets are delivered after a short delay. Still, most smile sheets are delivered just before learners leave the classroom or exit their elearning program.

Is this a problem? Yes, very much so! When learning is top-of-mind, learners can easily remember what they've learned and imagine themselves implementing their learning back on the job. But, unfortunately, such intentions are rarely transferred back to the workplace, so learners' responses on end-of-training smile sheets are extremely biased. Learners may think the training they received was effective—even when it was not.

We've already talked about the research that shows that learners are overly optimistic about their ability to remember what they've learned. They are likely to shun needed practice and repetitions because they can't think beyond the learning situation. They can't imagine what it will be like—cognitively—when their learning is not top-of-mind. As the researchers Dina Ghodsian, Robert Bjork, and Aaron Benjamin point out:

> *Trainees' performance during training is an unreliable indicator of posttraining performance. [Training designs] that enhance performance during training can yield poor long-term post-training performance, and other [training designs] that seem to create difficulties and slow the rate of learning can be optimal in terms of long-term performance. (1997, p. 63)*

Both learners and those who facilitate learning can be fooled by this paradox. When we're in a learning situation, we might feel we have learned fully—or it might seem like our learners have learned fully. But those feelings are poor indicators of whether the learning will carry through to future situations. Learners may feel a high level of confidence during learning, but their perceptions during learning can fool them into thinking that they will always have the learned information at the top of their minds. Alas, our cognitive machinery is simply not set up to allow us to imagine what our future cognitive states will feel like. Here's why: The state of our working memory is dependent on the environmental and cognitive cues influencing it in every moment. The cues during learning will always be different from the cues during a later performance—at the very least, they will be sufficiently different to elicit different working-memory states. Learners cannot predict their performance futures with enough specificity to predict whether they'll be able to remember or not.

Earlier, I argued—rather vociferously—that we need to help our learners make unbiased decisions when they complete our smile sheets. Unfortunately, almost nothing adds to smile-sheet bias more than deploying our smile sheets when learning is top-of-mind. When we give learners smile sheets immediately after learning, much of what they learned is highly accessible in memory; therefore, much of their perspective will be biased at that time toward what they recently learned.

But let's be careful here! While this top-of-mind condition makes it more difficult for learners to imagine their future cognitive states, measuring learners soon after learning does make it easier for learners to remember their recent state of mind. They are more likely to recall the feelings they had within training, their sense of comprehension, the difficulty they had in understanding new material, and their current levels of confidence and conviction. This is why it would be a mistake just to give learners smile sheets after a delay. There is a ton of rich information we would miss.

Let me be specific about the forgetting that can come with the timing of smile sheets. Even short delays of a few hours may produce enough forgetting that learners can't make good decisions on their smile sheets. For example, if learners are taught ten key concepts in a one-day workshop, by the end of the day—when they are answering smile-sheet questions—they may need a reminder about the topics they learned in the morning. For multiple-day training events, failing to remember can be even worse. Smile sheets that are delivered a day or more after learning should include some mechanism to remind the learners of the topics they learned and the methods used in the training.

In essence, the timing of smile sheets is open to two potent forces. One of these forces controls what learners remember—and hence what insights they can bring to smile-sheet decision making. The other influences learners' predictions of the future, also affecting decision making on smile sheets. To be clear, these forces are the following:

1. Learners will tend to remember and think about the most recent learning experiences and forget to consider earlier learning experiences.

2. Learners will be overconfident that (a) they will be able to remember and (b) they will remain motivated to apply what they've learned in their future workplace situations.

In balancing these competing forces in regard to the timing of smile sheets, we can help our learners make good smile sheet decisions by doing the following:

- Provide smile-sheet questions *soon after each topic area* to ensure learners can give us good feedback about their within-learning thoughts and feelings.

- Provide smile-sheet questions *after a delay* to ensure that learners can give us good feedback about how well the learning prepared them to remember.

- Provide smile-sheet questions *after learners have attempted to apply* what they've learned so that we get information about job relevance.

- Provide *reminders to learners about the details of the topics* that they've learned before asking them to respond to smile-sheet questions—especially when there is some likelihood that the learners may have forgotten aspects of the learning.[12]

When we analyze our smile-sheet results, we should also put into perspective the kinds of information we can get from different timings of smile-sheet deployment. The timing of smile sheets dictates what information we will be able to capture. If we only measure immediately at the end of learning, we will fail to get good information about remembering and application. If we only measure after a delay, we will fail to get good information about immediate comprehension, confusion, enjoyment, and confidence. When we analyze our results, we must take smile-sheet timing into account so that we draw valid conclusions.

## The Smile-Sheet Context

Another bias inherent in smile-sheet practice involves the contextual cues that are present when smile sheets are delivered. When people are questioned at the end of a learning event, they are being questioned within the same context in which they learned. Unfortunately, as huge amounts of research have shown, memory retrieval is influenced by the contextual cues in one's environment.[13]

---

12  One caveat: If you are also testing memory or decision making directly, you will want to do this before you remind the learners of what they learned.

13  Research reviews of context-dependent memory: Bjork & Richardson-Klavehn (1989); Smith (1988); Smith & Vela (2001); Eich (1980); Roediger & Guynn (1996); Davies (1986). Context alignment is so fundamental that it has been codified in the "encoding-specificity" principle (Tulving & Thompson, 1973) and in the notion of "transfer-appropriate processing" (Bransford, Franks, Morris, & Stein, 1979) and "context-dependent memory" (Smith, 1988).

In short, it is easier for us to remember something if we attempt to retrieve it in the same situation in which we learned it than if we attempt to retrieve it in another situation. The cues in our environment will either support correct retrieval or push us toward inappropriate retrieval processing.

This concept can be difficult to grasp, but all of us have experienced context-dependent memory in our lives. When you meet someone you know, but meet them in a strange situation and can't remember their name or you can't remember where you know them from, you've experienced context-dependent memory. If you can't remember your ATM code until you see the ATM keypad, you've experienced context-dependent memory. But context-dependent memory happens all the time, not just in these most obvious situations. We are being primed and triggered every minute of every day by the contextual cues in our environment.

For most training events, the learning context is not the work context—so we have a mismatch between the two. While our learners may be able to retrieve a key concept in the learning context, they may not be able to retrieve it in the work context. This is why—from a learning design perspective—it is critical to present learners with realistic situations and prompt decision making of the kind they'll have to use on the job.

But we're not talking learning design here. We're talking smile-sheet design and deployment. In terms of smile sheets, we want the cues while learners are completing their smile sheets to support valid smile-sheet decision making. We want cues from the learning situation to remind learners of the full extent of the learning context. We also want cues related to learners' worksites to support learners in deciding how well the training facilitates actual on-the-job performance.

If you're new to the concept of contextual triggering, this may all seem strange at first. Have no worries. I'll make the repercussions of this obvious as we go forward.

## Likert-Like Scales Create Ambiguous Smile-Sheet Results

We've already seen how Likert-like questions don't allow learners to make good smile-sheet decisions. Now we'll see how they produce less-than-meaningful results.

Smile sheets that utilize Likert-like scales are almost always transformed into numbers—for example:

- Strongly Agree = 5

- Agree = 4

- Neither Agree Nor Disagree = 3

- Disagree = 2

- Strongly Disagree = 1

Then, these numbers are averaged over learners. So for example, a training class with 20 people might produce the following results on one of its questions: 5, 5, 5, 5, 5, 5, 5, 5, 5, 5, 4, 4, 4, 4, 4, 3, 3, 3, 2, 1. These numbers average 4.1.

It's time for reflection. Take a deep breath. Breathe in. Breathe out. Inhale fresh air. Exhale the impurities. Let's examine the air-brush blurring that we just witnessed.

We first start with the fuzzy adjectives from the Likert-like scale. "Strongly agree" is already removed from the statement it has judged. Next, we transmortify the fuzzy adjective into a number.[14] Next, we average the number, removing even more information. Finally, we may remove all the questions that were asked but one. "The course achieved an overall score of 4.1." Again, we are leaving out significant amounts of information.

It's hard to breathe out all the impurities from this appalling transmortification. The end result bears little relationship to the question that was originally asked. And yet, somehow, without even a hint of regret, we boldly share our averaged

---

14  Transmortify is an intentional misspelling of the word *transmogrify*, which means "to transform, especially in a surprising or magical manner." It's mortifying that we work in a profession that does this!

smile-sheet results with our senior stakeholders. You might remember our earlier discussion with CEO Julie. When she closely examined what her chief learning officer was telling her, she not only found that the numbers didn't add up but also that the whole logic of smile-sheet data handling was built on a faulty foundation. It's bad enough that we share this data with our senior leaders, but it's perhaps even more scandalous that we believe in our numbers—and make decisions based on them.

What the hell does a result of 3.7, 4.1, or 4.2 mean? With all our transmortification, it means almost nothing. And let's remember, these numbers were proven by our two meta-analyses *not* to be correlated with learning! But even if we could trace our blurry averages up the chain to the source of meaning, we are still looking at an isolated number. Let me try to make this clear using a sports analogy. Just like in sports, our numbers don't really mean anything if we can't compare those numbers to some other comparator—to some other number.

Our numbers are not like numbers in sports or business that actually mean what they say they mean. Our 4.2 isn't the same thing as a baseball pitcher with a 4.20 earned run average or a rugby player with 4.2 yards per carry. Those numbers have inherent meaning. Pitchers try to get lower earned run averages. Rugby players (and American football players) try to average more yards per carry. But even these numbers don't have full meaning unless they are compared to some other numbers. Is a pitcher with a 4.20 earned run average doing well, doing okay, or doing poorly? We simply can't know unless we compare those numbers to some other standard. If the league average is 4.30, then our pitcher's 4.20 is about average. If the league's top five pitchers average 3.10, then our 4.20 pitcher is not close to being the best.

One final point about drawing averages from our smile-sheet data—and this is somewhat technical. While most smile sheets are reported out as averages, or "means" as statisticians call them, it's actually a statistically questionable practice to use the mean when the data doesn't follow a normal distribution (the typical "bell curve" distribution). The problem is that an average tells us nothing about whether the data is skewed up or down or not at all. So, again, we see that traditional smile-sheet practices leave out valuable information.

Numbers—indeed all results—attain full meaning only when they are compared to something. They can be compared to previous results, to other current results, or to some standard. Smile sheets are often compared to the following:

- To our previous same-course results

- To our other current-course results

- To other companies' course results

- To some standard (for example, a 4.0 course-rating threshold)

Our comparisons give us the illusion that our numbers have meaning, but again we fool ourselves and our stakeholders. We've seen how these Likert-derived numbers have fuzzy meaning to begin with—so to compare our current numbers to our previous numbers or to our other current numbers or to other companies' numbers is an exercise in magical thinking. The alternative—comparing our numbers to some standard—may seem enticing, but how can we select an arbitrary standard based on fuzzy numbers? Is a 4.0 acceptable, but not a 3.9? If so, why is a 4.0 acceptable? Why? Why? Why?

What makes these comparisons even worse is that most training courses are poorly designed—lacking in support for remembering and lacking in support for on-the-job application, among other deficiencies. Yes, yes, yes; there are excellent training courses. But most training courses are poorly designed. Comparing our courses to typical, poorly designed courses—even if our courses get seemingly good smile-sheet ratings—is deeply flawed and warrants a torrent of tears for our profession—and for our credibility as well.

The bottom line is that Likert-like scales on smile sheets produce inherently meaningless information. Correction: they produce information that is not only inherently meaningless but also inherently dangerous when it is taken seriously. It is dangerous because we are likely to make decisions based on the information, and our decisions will then be untouched by the factors that really matter for learning.

I've seen the danger of faulty smile-sheet data many times in my work as a consultant. Here's how it typically goes. I'm called in by a chief learning officer (or other senior learning leader). For this example, we'll make the person a CLO named Eugene. Eugene knows that a lot of his company's training is not nearly as effective as it could be. Eugene calls me in to do a learning audit, and I too find that by and large the training is poorly designed—so Eugene isn't imagining the problems. He'd like to make big changes, but his stakeholders—including his company's senior managers and, sadly enough, a large group of his own training staff—do not see the need for improvement. They point to the smile-sheet results that show that the training is routinely averaging 4.5s on a 5-point scale. Eugene is stuck! He's absolutely immobilized. He can nibble around the edges, making minor improvements, but he can't get the political support or organizational resources to make his company's training effective. Is there a way out for Eugene? Yes! He can fix the smile sheets!

Remember Julie, the CEO in my first example? If she had smile-sheet results that showed that her company's training courses were not supporting on-the-job performance, do you think she'd be satisfied with the status quo? If Eugene worked for her, you could bet he'd get the resources and support he'd need to create effective learning interventions.

Questions that use Likert-like scales are not the only questions that produce fuzzy information. Regardless of the types of answer choices we use, we must do everything in our power to avoid questions that produce bogus data.

## Traditional Smile-Sheet Questions

Perhaps the most important biases in smile-sheet design are the questions themselves. Let's do a thought experiment. If we asked only about the quality of the room, breaks, and food of a training session, learners would be biased toward providing data on those criteria. Even if we added open-ended questions after these triggering questions, learners would focus more on the room, breaks, and food than on other aspects of the training. That's probably obvious, but what isn't so obvious is that the questions we ask aren't always the ones that target the most important factors. Most smile sheets simply ask the wrong questions. They don't ask questions that are related to learning factors of importance. They don't take into account the latest research on how learning should be designed. They don't parley that knowledge into a smile-sheet design that would index training on the factors that matter most. In the next chapter, we'll look in-depth at the factors that smile sheets should be assessing.

## Summary: The Stink of Traditional Smile Sheets

On our smile sheets, we want the learners to be able to make good decisions, and we want to send clear messages about what they have decided. Anything that fuzzes things up hurts the validity of the smile-sheet data. We've seen that Likert-like scales fail to provide meaningful data, that our transmogrifications distort reality, that our traditional methods are prone to bias. To put it simply, we have to do better than this.

Our final autopsy report on traditional smile sheets reads as follows:

1. Death by a thousand cuts.

2. Research on traditional smile sheets finds that they are unrelated to learning results.

3. Subjective responses are not carefully analyzed to minimize their most damaging effects.

4. Likert-like responses hurt learners' decision making as they respond.

5. Likert-like responses are transmogrified inappropriately, losing information.

6. Likert-like responses produce unclear guidance for action.

7. Numerical averaging of smile-sheet data is inappropriate and conveys results in a way that hurts stakeholder decision making.

8. The timing of smile sheets introduces bias.

9. The context of smile-sheet deployment introduces bias.

10. Smile-sheet questions focus on factors that are only weakly related to learning.

# CHAPTER 3

## SMILE SHEETS SHOULD PREDICT TRAINING EFFECTIVENESS

T RADITIONAL SMILE SHEETS ARE failing us. It's time we change that and design a smile sheet that works. To do that, we must determine what a smile sheet should do and then build it from the ground up.

Before we begin, however, we have to answer an important question. *"Dr. T, if smile sheets are not correlated with learning—and if they have so many design flaws—shouldn't we just avoid smile sheets altogether?"* Well, that's a very good question. Let me answer it in three ways. First, even poorly de-signed smile sheets can occasionally produce valuable insights—especially if open-ended comments are allowed that provide deeper insights than multiple-choice questions. Second, let's be real. Just because smile sheets are obvious-ly flawed doesn't mean they will be quickly replaced with better evaluations. In the near future, the weight of tradition and expectations will keep most or-ganizations using smile sheets. Given this, we'll probably have more success in improving smile sheets than in proselytizing their abandonment. Finally, if we start from scratch—using research-inspired wisdom about learning—we can certainly design a more effective smile sheet. In this chapter, I aim to prove that to you.

Many of the most venerated thinkers in learning measurement have ar-gued that in the Kirkpatrick Model, Level 1 reactions are like a customer-sat-isfaction survey: they tell us whether people are satisfied with their learning events. They further argue that Level 1, learner satisfaction, is related to Level 2, learning; Level 3, behavior-change; and Level 4, organization results. This equates to the following: If learners aren't happy with the learning event, they won't learn anything and learning will not have a positive impact. But as we saw previously from the two research meta-analyses, this argument is wrong. Sometimes satisfaction is related to learning. Sometimes it isn't. We must go beyond the notion of customer satisfaction to look at the factors that enable learning. It is simply not enough for a smile sheet to focus on learner satisfaction—or other less-critical learning goals.

What, then, should smile sheets do? They should do two things. First, smile sheets should give us a good gauge of the likelihood that the learning has utilized factors that are actually essential to learning. Second, smile sheets should produce results that are actionable—that send clear messages about the success or failure of the learning design and deployment. Let me highlight these two key goals for an effective smile sheet.

### *A Maximally Effective Smile Sheet*

1. **Gauges the effectiveness of the training design**
   Answering the question, "Will the training be effective in supporting on-the-job performance?"

2. **Enables reporting that is actionable**
   Answering the question, "Will the smile-sheet results communicate with clarity and urgency to guide action?"

## Measuring the Inputs and Outputs

Before we go on to see how we can redesign our smile sheets, it's important that I share a fundamental concept in learning measurement. Learning interventions can be evaluated based on their outputs and their inputs. The following lists should give you a good idea of the difference.

Examples of Inputs

- Costs of development

- Instructional-design methods used

- Supervisor support for training and on-the-job learning

- Senior-management support for learning

- Time spent in learning

Examples of Outputs

- Number of people trained

- Learner's satisfaction levels

- Results of multiple-choice tests

- Results of scenario-based decision making

- Results of simulation exercises

- Job-performance improvements

- Organizational results (examples: lower costs, higher productivity)

Ultimately, what we care about is whether our learning interventions produce results—that their outputs provide benefits at a reasonable cost-benefit ratio. But not all outputs are equally important. The number of people trained and the levels of learner satisfaction are not very useful. What is critical is (a) whether learners have understood what we taught them, (b) whether they remember what we taught them, and (c) whether they've successfully applied what we taught them.

Smile sheets don't capture—and can't fully capture—these important learning outcomes. Thus—and this is *extremely critical*—smile sheets should not be used in isolation. They must be augmented with outcome measures that get at (a) learner understanding, (b) learner remembering, and (c) learner application. This doesn't mean that every implementation of every course requires our most careful measurement methods, but it does require that we are measuring important outcomes enough to be getting good feedback.

Smile sheets can't fully capture these important outcome measures, but they can be designed to give us better predictions about these outcomes than have traditionally been available from smile sheets. By the end of this chapter, you'll have clear ideas about how to do this.

## Gauging the Effectiveness of Training Design

You'll remember that there are two factors that are critical to the design of a smile sheet, (1) gauging the effectiveness of the training design and (2) enabling reporting that is actionable. This chapter covers the first of these aspects—gauging the effectiveness of training design.

What does effective training look like? Effective training creates improved on-the-job performance.[15] It does *not* just create awareness or increased knowledge! Given this truism, it's helpful to distinguish between training that is meant to provide awareness and training that is meant to support actual performance improvement. The following three-level taxonomy makes this clear.

### *Levels of Training*

1. Awareness training

2. Performance training

3. Performance training with performance assistance

*Awareness training* conveys information to learners but doesn't provide sufficient support for remembering or on-the-job application. Awareness training

---

15  For those of you in education who aren't immediately concerned with learners' job performance but do want to create better student-reaction forms—you'll have to insert some other performance outcome every time I talk about on-the-job performance. The principle is still the same. You don't teach just to educate. You teach so that your learners will do something different at some later time. What is it that you want them to be able to do? In what situations will this behavior be utilized? Once you answer those questions, you'll know your performance outcomes.

does not ensure that the learning will be applied on the job.[16] *Performance training* provides remembering and application support—and aims specifically to improve on-the-job performance. By augmenting performance training with *performance assistance* at the worksite, we can accelerate the journey to full performance proficiency.[17]

Here's how a course on the same topic might look at each of the three levels. Let's take as an example a one-day course on how to provide good customer service in a hardware store.

1.  **Example of awareness training**

    The awareness training course is composed mostly of lecture. It talks about the importance of good customer service to the hardware store business. It tries to motivate learners to engage the learning with attention. It reviews the rules of good customer service. It provides examples. It asks the learners to reflect on the examples and discuss bad customer service experiences they might have had as a customer. It encourages learners to create action plans, listing what goals they have for customer service when they return to the job.

2.  **Example of performance training**

    The performance-training course is composed of one-third lecture and two-thirds practice, feedback, and more practice. It provides many of the topics that the awareness training course provides, but shortens them by more than half. It provides learners with a two-page job aid of sixteen critical customer service situations and suggestions for how to handle those situations. Each of the sixteen situations is first role-played using the job aid and is followed by peer feedback and discussion. Learners then write their own set of

---

16  Awareness training also includes read-and-acknowledge training, where a document is presented to learners and they are asked to read and acknowledge that they understand it and/or will comply with it.

17  I use the term *performance assistance* rather than *performance support* because many people view performance support as tool-based support and I want to include human-based support as well.

actions for each of the situations in the spaces provided on the job aid form. Learners role-play each of the sixteen situations, referring to their job aid only if they need it. They get feedback and revise their action plans if warranted. Learners are then presented with more complex customer service scenarios and act out their responses, get feedback, and reflect on what they've learned. Finally, learners learn to handle common obstacles they may face in implementing their new learning.

3. **Example of performance training with performance assistance**
   For this version of the course, learners receive performance training as described above, but in addition, their workplace is prepared for their posttraining application of the course material. This is done by (a) preparing the hardware store managers to model and coach the desired behaviors, (b) encouraging learner-manager discussions before the course even starts, (c) providing an after-training application plan for the learner and a coaching plan for the manager, (d) evaluating actual customer service results in a manner that gives both managers and learners corrective feedback, (e) reminding learners and managers of the key points of the program periodically after the training ends, and (f) acknowledging effort and success as learners and managers apply what they've learned.

Awareness training is not very effective from a learning standpoint. It simply doesn't provide enough support to ensure that learners can remember or apply what they've learned. In their recent research review in the top-tier scientific journal *Psychological Science in the Public Interest,* Eduardo Salas, Scott Tannenbaum, Kurt Kraiger, and Kimberly Smith-Jentsch (2012) reviewed the research on training and development and highlighted the weaknesses of awareness training.

*Recent reports suggest that information and demonstrations (i.e., workbooks, lectures, and videos) remain the strategies of choice in industry. And this is a problem [because] we know from the body of research that learning occurs through the practice and feedback components. . . . It has long been recognized that traditional, stand-up lectures are an inefficient and unengaging strategy for imparting new knowledge and skills.* (p. 86)

Our goal as training professionals, then, should be performance training or performance training augmented with on-the-job performance assistance. Certainly, some circumstances warrant awareness training, but these are few. After all, if we're not impacting performance, what have we achieved? In almost all cases, we should target performance training as our minimum standard.

Okay, let's take a breath here. I just took time to digress into a discussion of the three levels of training. I did this for two reasons. First, this three-tier distinction is one of the most important distinctions in training and development (not that many people think about it this way), and I wanted to make sure that you could become one of the enlightened ones. Do you feel enlightened? Second, I offer this discussion because I want to highlight the main point of this chapter—that one of the goals of smile-sheet design is that we ought to be gauging the effectiveness of our training. Awareness training is generally *not* effective, performance training is effective, and performance training with performance assistance is maximally effective.

## Two Models of Training Effectiveness

Now, I'm going to introduce two models that will take us deeper into the discussion of what makes training effective.

The Training Maximizers Model offers a good way to begin thinking about what effective performance training looks like.

**Whereas successful awareness training only requires (B) engaging learning events and (C) support for basic understanding, performance training requires a healthy dose of all the Training Maximizers.**

Performance training requires all of the Training Maximizers listed in the figure, whereas awareness training tends to focus only on B (creating engaging learning events) and C (providing support for basic understanding of the concepts to be learned). The Training Maximizers Model is based on years of research of the kind I have compiled from top-tier, refereed scientific journals in building the Decisive Dozen, a list of the most important learning factors.

The Decisive Dozen are worth exploring in more depth—so you can see the kinds of factors that really matter in learning.[18] I like to think of the Decisive

---

18   To learn more about the Decisive Dozen, see www.is.gd/ddResearch.

Dozen in terms of the way biologists think of DNA. The human genome consists of 23 pairs of chromosomes with approximately 23,000 protein-coding genes and slightly more than three billion DNA base pairs. The human genome enables us to live, but some parts of the genome are more important than other parts. Consider that chimpanzees and bonobos share 99% of the same genome as humans. Clearly, that 1% difference is everything to us! Indeed, scientists have used the term *junk DNA* to indicate that a large portion of DNA has little or no purpose.

The learning genome is the same. Of the thousands of learning factors we might consider, some are sine-qua-non essential. Some have moderate importance. Most have little importance. I spent more than a decade sifting through the scientific research on learning, memory, and instruction—trying to discover the most important factors in the learning genome. I ended up with twelve indispensable factors.

Certainly, there may be others I've missed, or other ways to present the factors that I've compiled, but my commitment to these twelve factors rests on this assurance: when we use these twelve factors to design learning interventions, we will be creating learning interventions that are better than 95% of those deployed today.[19]

I started my research and consulting practice, Work-Learning Research, in 1998 because I saw us as an industry jumping from one fad to another and holding on sanctimoniously to learning approaches that didn't work well or at all. If you've been in the learning field for any amount of time—whether its workplace learning or K–12 education—you certainly must have noticed how

---

19  Such a bold statement demands evidence. But this is easy. Most workplace learning interventions do not utilize very many repetitions of key learning points—and yet research shows that just a few repetitions can increase learning by 100% or more. Most workplace learning interventions do not utilize very many realistic practice opportunities—and yet research demonstrates that retrieval practice is better than simple repetitions by up to 100% or more, and aligning the learning context with the retrieval context can improve results up to 50% (the context alignment is what we mean by "realistic" practice). Because most learning interventions don't give enough retrieval practice, they don't give enough feedback—and the feedback they do give is often poorly designed to be too lengthy, too immediate, and not corrective enough. Giving learners feedback properly can improve learning results easily by 50% or more. Of course, my 95% prediction is a quick-and-dirty estimate, but I hope my point is clear. Most workplace learning interventions are not currently well designed—you can easily do better by following the Decisive Dozen learning factors.

learning fads come and go with the breeze. The Decisive Dozen is my answer to this—an anchor to keep us from flying hither and thither in the wind.[20]

Here are the elements of the Decisive Dozen:

## Basic Enablers

1.  *Content*
    When learners learn, they ought to learn from content that is correct and true and relevant to their future needs.

2.  *Exposure*
    When learners have a need to learn, they must be exposed to relevant or targeted learning content or learning events.

## Creating Engagement and Understanding

3.  *Guiding Attention*
    When we guide learners' attention to the most critical information or contextual stimuli, their learning improves.

4.  *Creating Correct Conceptions*
    When we structure learning so that learners can quickly build correct understanding, they learn more effectively and more efficiently.

5.  *Repetition*
    When we provide repetitions (in a manner that engages), learners more effectively understand and remember.

6.  *Feedback*
    When we utilize feedback appropriately, we correct learners' misconceptions and support correct retrieval.

---

20  I'll credit Edgar Allan Poe for this use of "hither and thither." "The Conqueror Worm," http://www.poetryfoundation.org/poem/178359.

7.  *Variation*
    When we vary the learning materials, proper contingencies can be learned, future memory retrieval is improved, and learners stay more engaged with the learning content.

## Supporting Remembering

8.  *Context Alignment*
    When we integrate workplace cues (or other task-relevant cues) in our learning events, future memory retrievals are more likely to be triggered (and triggered when needed).

9.  *Retrieval Practice*
    When we provide practice in memory retrieval, learners are more likely in future circumstances to have successful memory retrieval of the information learned.

10. *Spacing*
    When we space repetitions of content and instructional events over time, future memory retrieval is improved.

## Enabling Future Application

11. *Persuasion*
    When we persuade learners, they will be more likely to reinforce the concepts learned—and engage in attempts to use what they have learned in their work and in their lives.

12. *Perseverance*
    When we support our learners in persevering in both learning and in subsequent learning application, we enable them to engage with goal-directed metacognitive effort.

When we focus on these twelve factors first, we will create better learning interventions. These factors are supported by hundreds—if not thousands—of scientific research studies.

*"But, Dr. Thalheimer, aren't we talking about learning measurement,* not *learning design?"* Damn right! It's time to get back to learning measurement!

The point I'm trying to reinforce by sharing the Decisive Dozen and the Training Maximizers Model is that when we create a smile sheet, it should give us an idea of whether the training program will be effective in improving on-the-job performance—and when we're doing that, shouldn't we base our learning-measurement designs on learning research? While the Decisive Dozen is a list of learning factors, the Training Maximizers Model is a process model—one that aligns with the research that underpins the Decisive Dozen. Whereas each of the seven Training Maximizers process steps provides you, as a learning designer, a specific goal to achieve (for example, supporting remembering), the Decisive Dozen learning factors provide you with the ingredient list you can use (for example, retrieval practice) to achieve those goals.

The bottom line here is that before we start thinking about how to design our new smile sheet, we have to begin with an understanding of what we're trying to accomplish in terms of our training. Both the Decisive Dozen and the Training Maximizers Model are offered here to make us sensitive to what good training looks like.

## Four Pillars of Training Effectiveness

Now that we've reflected on what good training looks like, what's the next step in creating an effective smile sheet? My recommendation begins below. First, it may be helpful to remind you of the two primary goals of Performance-Focused Smile Sheets, the first of which is the focus of this chapter:

- Gauge the effectiveness of the training design

- Enable reporting that is actionable

If one of our primary goals in creating a smile sheet is to determine whether a learning program creates on-the-job performance, our secondary goals should be the following, which I will refer to as the four pillars of training effectiveness.

1. Do the learners understand?

2. Will they remember?

3. Are they motivated to apply?

4. Are there after-training supports in place?

If a training program achieves all four of these goals, it is extremely likely to create on-the-job performance. Of course, this assumes that the content is valid and relevant.[21]

We will now look at each of the four secondary goals in turn.

### *Learners Understand*

Obviously, learners must correctly comprehend the content they are learning. While the best way to measure such comprehension is with tests of learning—not with smile sheets—smile sheets can give the learners' perceptions of whether they understand the material, which, in general, is a reasonable proxy for their understanding.

Third-level (or tertiary) goals related to learner understanding include such things as making sure the learners are engaged in the learning and making sure they are provided with the cognitive supports they need to fully comprehend the information. Cognitive supports can include such things as advance organizers, aligning to prior knowledge, animations, examples, use of white space, clear writing, and comprehension testing and feedback.

Fourth-level (or quaternary) goals related to learner understanding include such things as ensuring learners are motivated to learn; the classroom environment is conducive to learning; the instructors are credible, engaging, and supportive; the learning is well organized; and the learners are satisfied with the learning experience. Note that these fourth-level goals—a long way

---

21   The question of content validity and relevance—as portrayed in both the Decisive Dozen and the Training Maximizers Model—is not one of the secondary goals because smile sheets can't get at the truth of content validity and relevance. Although learners can give their perceptions of these factors, learners are not always reliable sources on these issues.

removed from the actual effectiveness of the training—are typically what are targeted by smile sheets. While often smile sheets do ask about the third-level goals of learners' engagement and belief in the value of the concepts, all too often traditional smile sheets focus on fourth-level goals such as instructor competence, the learning environment, the organization of the learning, and overall learner satisfaction—failing to look at other key tertiary goals and completely ignoring secondary goals that actually indicate meaningful impact. It is no wonder that our traditional smile sheets are ineffective in providing us with good feedback.

### Learners Remember

Having learners understand is a good thing, but it is not sufficient. If we don't help our learners remember what they've learned, then we have failed them. Too many learning interventions fall short in this regard. Our learners can't apply what they've learned if they can't remember what they've learned.

The best way to measure remembering is with delayed tests of learning— not with smile sheets—but our smile sheets can be designed to give us indications of whether the learning is likely to lead to remembering.

Third-level goals related to remembering include whether the learners have received realistic practice, repetitions spaced over time, and situation-action triggers to spur spontaneous remembering. As laid out in the Decisive Dozen, long-term remembering is supported by aligning the learning and performance contexts, by providing learners with significant levels of retrieval practice, and by spacing repetitions of key learning messages over time. Without these supports, learners are unlikely to remember what they've learned.

### Learners Are Motivated to Apply What They've Learned

Mostly, when we learning professionals think of motivation, we think of the learners' motivation to engage in learning. Equally important is our learners' motivation to apply what they've learned. Let's face the truth. Learning that truly changes behavior usually requires substantial motivation and metacognitive effort. Learners not only have to remember what they've learned but they also need to initiate actions in their jobs—in between the flow and bounce of regular practices. Getting started may be the biggest obstacle, but learners then have to persevere in the face of obstacles, other priorities, and the deadening weight of tradition and culture. Learners have to race time before they forget what they learned—or they have to remind themselves of what they learned. They have to ensure that they prioritize the application of their learning—and reprioritize it as other demands take precedent. To navigate these many issues, learners have to go back to their jobs with substantial motivation and maintain their motivation over time.

Third-level goals related to motivation-to-apply include whether the learners have a belief in the concepts they learned, whether they have a sense of self-efficacy in being able to apply their new skills successfully, and whether they feel they can continue to learn and improve their new skills on the job. Training that does not address these motivational imperatives is unlikely to lead to successful transfer to the job.

### After-Training Supports Are in Place

Not only do learners need to be motivated to apply what they've learned but concrete supports should be available to learners to help them navigate the flotsam of implementation. While some rare learners will rise up and implement their learning without support, a large majority will be successful only if they have additional resources and guidance.

Third-level goals related to after-training support include whether the learners have been inoculated (while in training) to the obstacles they might face, whether they've been given sufficient practice (while in training) regarding what can go wrong, whether they've been given job aids (and practiced using them while in training), and whether supervisors are likely to follow up with resources, encouragement, and guidance.

## Summary: How to Gauge Training Effectiveness

One of the primary goals of a smile sheet is to assess whether a training program is likely to be effective. Training programs should go beyond awareness training to performance training, ideally augmented with performance assistance. The Training Maximizers Model does a nice job of conveying—without a level of complexity that might overwhelm—much of the research regarding what makes training effective. These factors can be distilled—for the purpose of smile-sheet design—into the four pillars of training effectiveness, which I outlined above: (1) understanding, (2) remembering, (3) motivation to apply, and (4) after-training supports. These second-level smile-sheet goals are aligned with third-level goals that can also be targeted for smile-sheet measurement. If our smile sheet is going to provide reasonable information about whether a training program is going to be successful, it must ask questions that get at the secondary and tertiary goals outlined above. It won't always be easy to do that, but it is possible.

Because these new smile sheets are specifically designed to assess the likelihood of on-the-job performance improvement, I have labeled them Performance-Focused Smile Sheets. They won't be perfect in ascertaining whether a training program can lead to performance, but they will be significantly better than traditional smile sheets.

Finally, let me remind you of one of my main points. Smile sheets are not perfect and should not be used alone. However, given that most organizations will continue to use them, we should at least use smile sheets that are effective in providing us with performance-relevant information.

# CHAPTER 4

# SMILE SHEETS SHOULD PRODUCE ACTIONABLE RESULTS

IN THE PREVIOUS CHAPTER, we covered the first imperative of a smile sheet—gauging the likelihood that training will be effective in producing on-the-job performance improvement. In this chapter, we will cover the second imperative of smile sheets: that they produce results that are actionable. When our smile-sheet results are actionable, they communicate with clarity and urgency about whether a training program should be kept, modified, or discarded; moreover, they guide us to see what design elements should be improved.

There are four sets of guidelines that will enable us to create actionable results:

1. The quality of learners' smile-sheet decisions

2. Whether smile-sheet results distinguish between different levels of success

3. Whether we are measuring the things that matter

4. Whether we are using the smile-sheet opportunity to educate our stakeholders

Each will be discussed in turn.

## Quality of Learners' Smile-Sheet Decisions

First and foremost, our smile-sheet design and deployment methods should help learners make good decisions in answering the smile-sheet questions. It is critical that we prevent the garbage-in, garbage-out problem. If learner's smile-sheet efforts produce poor data, then any reports we create will be garbage. If learners don't take smile sheets seriously, if they are rushing through the questions, if they are overly fatigued, they won't give their full attention to answering the questions, and their responses won't reflect their most accurate judgments. If learners can't remember what they learned or can't remember the specifics of the learning events, they won't be able to make accurate assessments of their learning. If learners are guided to unimportant criteria and distracted from critical learning factors, their responses won't fully reflect the most important factors. If answer choices don't provide clarity or enough granularity to help learners make distinctions between the options, then accuracy will be harmed. If leading questions—or other biasing questions—are included, then learners' responses will be biased.

As you can see, there are many ways that learners' smile-sheet decisions can be biased or inaccurate. Here are some recommended guidelines for avoiding these dangers:

> 1. *Remind learners of the learning experience.*
>    Unless the learning event is very short (less than an hour) and smile sheets are presented soon after learning, learners should be reminded of the topics presented and the learning methods employed. Otherwise, the learners will be making smile-sheet decisions based only on the most salient aspects of the training, ignoring the bulk of the training experience. Reminding learners of what they learned can be a tricky proposition because it can lengthen the smile sheet and make it feel unwieldy. Reminding can consist of a list of the learning topics presented to learners before they answer smile-sheet questions. Or, the topics themselves can be integrated into the smile sheets as questions. For example, questions could ask the learners to rate each topic on its relevance to their job or ask them to pick out the three most important topics. Of course, reminding need not be incorporated into the smile

sheet. If learners review the material in some way, or are given a test on the training concepts immediately before the smile sheet, such events can serve as reminders as well. The one caveat is that if these reminders are not hard-wired into the process, then comparing the smile-sheet results from one class to another will not be a fair comparison, as different instructors will provide different levels of reminding.

2. *Increase learner attention.*

To improve learners' attention as they answer smile-sheet questions, a persuasive and personal appeal should be made to learners about the importance of the smile-sheet results. Smile sheets should not be too long or too short. If they are too long, learners will become fatigued and disinterested. If they are too short, learners will get the message that the smile sheets are not important. Within a few weeks after the training, trainers or instructional designers should follow up with learners to let them know how the training course has been improved (or at least evaluated) with the recent smile-sheet results. Smile-sheet questions should be carefully designed. By using well-designed questions, learners are more likely to take smile sheets seriously. Questions should use descriptive answer choices—not Likert-like scales. Likert-like scales just don't feel very important. Ample time should be given for smile-sheet completion. Moreover, it can be valuable to offer a learning interaction after the smile sheets are completed so that the smile sheets are not the very last thing to be completed as learners run out the door.

3. *Avoid biasing questions.*

Care must be given not to lead learners in one direction or another with the question stems or with the answer choices. For example, avoid affirmations such as the following: "My skills and abilities improved as a result of this training." These types of affirmations push learners to answer in the affirmative. Similarly, avoid answer choices that lead to bias. This is obvious for some sets of answer choices, but not for others. You'll want to ensure that you provide answer choices that are equally positive and negative, and/or that encompass the full range of possibilities that might be expected. If you have doubts about whether your smile-sheet questions are creating bias, seek a measurement expert. In fact, you probably ought to seek a measurement expert anyway, because you're unlikely to see your own biases—unless you're incredibly experienced.

4. *Ask clear and relevant questions.*
One of the rules of measurement is never to ask a question whose answer can't or won't be used to actually make some kind of improvement. For example, don't ask about the quality of the diagnostic instruments used in a course if your organization is unlikely to change them. Similarly, don't ask questions about low-priority issues, for example, the quality of the food or the cleanliness of the restrooms. If low-priority topics are a real issue, learners will write about them in open-ended questions. Finally, make sure the wording is crystal clear. Fuzzy wording makes it hard for learners to interpret. For example, the following question stem could be worded more clearly: "I was well engaged during the learning event." The problem is that "well engaged" could have many meanings. It could connote attention, enjoyment, activity, or something else. To be more specific we might write, "My attention did not wander during the training session."

5. *Ask questions that learners can answer knowledgeably.*
Sometimes we ask questions with good intent, but without asking ourselves whether the learners are likely to be good judges of the issue queried. Here's an example of a question that learners are unlikely to answer with insight: "My learning was enhanced by the course structure." Learners are likely to be unaware of how the course structure affects their learning. Here's another one: "I was able to relate each of the learning objectives to the learning I achieved." This question will not only be difficult to answer, but it's largely irrelevant to whether the learning event was successful.

It makes little difference whether learners relate their learning to a learning objective or not. This issue falls within the junk DNA of the learning genome.

6. ***Provide descriptive and easily understood answer choices.***
Learners will make better decisions if we use descriptive answers rather than Likert-like response choices. Of course, our descriptive answers have to be well crafted, which is not always easy. Shorter answers are more easily comprehended, but sometimes more words are required to be precise. The right balance is needed.

7. ***Provide delayed smile sheets.***
Smile sheets delivered to learners in their worksites two to four weeks after the training can provide information that end-of-training smile sheets cannot provide. Specifically, delayed smile sheets help learners see whether they've actually implemented the new material or not. Moreover, they can help provide information about the obstacles and success factors that hurt or helped implementation of the learning. This doesn't mean that immediate smile sheets should be avoided—a point I'll expound on in Chapter 7, which focuses on delayed smile sheets.

## Distinguishing Between Different Levels of Success

Smile-sheet results should distinguish between different levels of success. In other words, when someone reviews the smile-sheet results, those results should clearly differentiate between success and failure of the training and between different levels of success. Without clear lines of demarcation, we as learning professionals won't know what to do with the smile-sheet results. We won't know whether we need to keep things as they are, improve the current training methods, or do a complete rethinking of the training design. Similarly, our stakeholders won't really know what to make of the smile-sheet results either. Given that one of our responsibilities is to clearly convey our results to our organizational stakeholders, we have a responsibility to ensure that those results are actionable.

Here are some recommended guidelines:

1. ***Don't transform results into numbers.***
   Smile-sheet results should not be transformed into numbers, because numbers don't distinguish between success levels. There is no clear demarcation between a 3.8, 3.9, 4.0, 4.1, 4.2, and so on.

2. ***Avoid meaningless answer-choice labels.***
   Results that have relatively meaningless labels, such as "Strongly Agree," also provide no clear demarcation between levels of success. For example, it isn't clear whether "Strongly Agree" is the only acceptable result or whether "Agree" should be considered sufficient.

3. ***Delineate standards for each answer choice during question design.***
   One way to help you design your questions to enable different levels of success is to delineate the standards as you design each question. Let's examine the following question as an example:

---

**Now that you've taken the course, how well do you feel you understand the concepts taught in the course?**

   A. I have some significant CONFUSIONS AND/OR BLIND SPOTS.

   B. I have a BASIC FAMILIARITY with the concepts.

   C. I have a SOLID UNDERSTANDING of the concepts.

   D. I have a COMPREHENSIVE UNDERSTANDING of the concepts.

   E. I have an EXPERT-LEVEL UNDERSTANDING of the concepts.

---

Most organizations who use smile sheets do not have standards for responses, so if they used the question presented above, they would wait until they received learner responses before deciding what results would be acceptable and what results would not be acceptable. This after-the-fact analysis lends itself to bias, to multiple and conflicting interpretations, and to confusion about what to do.

The alternative is to specify the standards when the question is being designed. For example, the answer choices might have the following standards associated with them.

---

**Now that you've taken the course, how well do you feel you understand the concepts taught in the course?**

A. I have some significant CONFUSIONS AND/OR BLIND SPOTS.

*Standard: Unacceptable for any type of training program.*

B. I have a BASIC FAMILIARITY with the concepts.

*Standard: Unacceptable for performance-focused programs; Acceptable for awareness-focused programs.*

C. I have a SOLID UNDERSTANDING of the concepts.

*Standard: Acceptable result.*

D. I have a COMPREHENSIVE UNDERSTANDING of the concepts.

*Standard: Superior result.*

E. I have an EXPERT-LEVEL UNDERSTANDING of the concepts.

*Standard: Unlikely result, as expertise takes more than training.*

---

## Measuring Things That Matter

While I hinted at this in the previous section on the quality of the questions, this issue is worth highlighting separately. The simple principle is that we should measure things that matter—and we should avoid asking questions about things that are low priority or are of less relevance to actual training effectiveness.

The best way to measure things that matter is to commit to measuring the four pillars of training effectiveness: (1) understanding, (2) remembering, (3) motivation to apply, and (4) after-training supports. We've already covered this in the previous chapter, so there is no need to go into more depth here. One critical point, however, is that measuring training effectiveness—as much as the format of smile sheets allows—is the central guiding principle of Performance-Focused Smile Sheets.

## Educating Our Stakeholders

As workplace learning-and-performance professionals, our primary responsibility is to help people excel in their jobs. To meet this demanding responsibility, we have to parlay resources and know-how in a manner that coordinates among a vast number of people across our organizations. To manage this coordination, we have to persuade others. With severely limited touch points, we often find it difficult to persuade. Our efforts at educating our stakeholders often fall short—and when we fail to persuade, often learning and performance suffers.

Indeed, the most astute learning leaders make regular attempts to build relationships and educate key stakeholders about how learning can be used to bolster organizational performance. But even the best learning leaders can have difficulty in educating stakeholders.

One of the reasons we haven't been successful is that we rely too much on making good arguments. We rely too much on conscious channels of perception, even though these are less potent than unconscious channels and can easily be filtered out or ignored. Let me give you an example. If we want drivers to drive more slowly on city streets, we have two options: we can try to reach them with conscious messaging like speed-limit signs, or we can use subconscious triggers that prompt them to slow down. As traffic engineers have found, speed-limit signs don't work as well as subconscious triggers. For example, narrowing traffic lanes, planting trees close to the road, and getting rid of center lane lines send subconscious messages to drivers that prompt them to slow down. Trees, for instance, send an unconscious message that you're driving through a residential area where there might be pedestrians, dogs, and children playing.

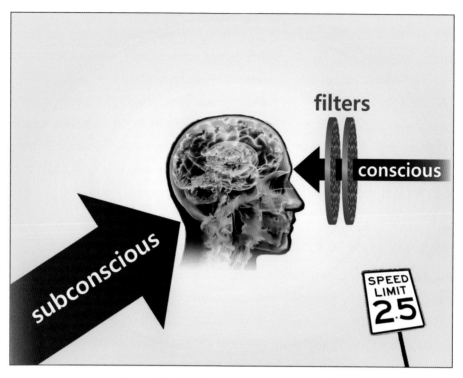

**Speed-limit signs are not as powerful
as subconscious traffic-calming methods.**

Fortunately, we do have another option besides conscious messaging. We can use "stealth messaging" as a way to persuade and educate. Stealth messages are messages that are conveyed during our routine practices and procedures. For example, suppose we are serious about being performance-focused and we want to create more training programs that are performance-focused. We could try to educate our stakeholders through ordinary means, by creating well-designed PowerPoint presentations, by stating our case in meetings, and/or by writing memos and reports that convey our performance-focused message. Alternatively, we could use stealth messages within our recruiting, evaluation, reporting, and other standard operating procedures.

Smile sheets are one of the most important practices we engage in—in terms of sending messages to key stakeholders in our organizations, that is. The results are seen by senior managers of all sorts and by trainers, instructional designers, and learning leaders. Traditional smile sheets send weak and confusing messages, but Performance-Focused Smile Sheets can send critical messages about whether our courses have sufficient support for remembering, after-training follow-through, appropriate job aids, supervisory support for learning, and so forth. By designing better smile sheets, we can send stealth messages that are potent and are less likely to be filtered out.

Being able to send potent stealth messages requires us to follow the recommendations discussed so far—and it requires us to do an effective job of developing reports and presenting them to our key stakeholders. Chapter 8 will focus on how to report out the smile-sheet results. The next chapter provides a look at specific smile-sheet questions.

## Summary: How to Produce Actionable Results

Traditional smile sheets often leave us in an unconscious state of indecision. We are lulled into a mesmerizing complacency, not even knowing that we ought to be making improvements to our learning interventions. In short, too many of today's smile sheets do not, and cannot, guide action. They do nothing to help us create virtuous cycles of continuous improvement. They leave us in the dark.

Fortunately, there are a number of actions we can take to ensure that our smile sheets produce actionable results. At the highest conceptual level, we need to help our learners make better smile-sheet decisions, we have to design our questions to distinguish between success and failure, we have to measure factors that relate to learning effectiveness, and we have to design our smile sheets so that they send appropriate stealth messages to our key stakeholders, including ourselves. In this chapter, we highlighted the following key design and deployment recommendations:

1.  Remind learners of the content and the learning experience to ensure they consider the full learning experience.

2.  Persuade learners to attend to smile sheets with full engagement.

3.  Ensure smile sheets are not too long and are not too short.

4.  Follow up with learners to let them know that the smile-sheet results were reviewed and utilized in redesign.

5.  Use descriptive answer choices. Do not use numbers, fuzzy adjectives, or other vague wording.

6.  Avoid using affirmations in your questions.

7.  Use answer choices that have a balance between positive and negative responses.

8.  Use answer choices that offer the full range of choices that might be expected.

9.  Seek a measurement expert to check your question wording to help you avoid biases and unclear language.

10. Never ask a question that you can't or won't be able to use to make an improvement.

11. Don't ask learners questions that they won't be good at answering.

12. Balance the length and precision of your answer choices—keeping the answers as short as possible, but lengthening them as needed to make them precise enough so that learners know what they mean.

13. Provide delayed smile sheets in addition to in-the-learning smile sheets.

14. Do not transform smile-sheet results into numbers.

15. Delineate standards of success and failure—acceptable results versus unacceptable results—in advance of training.

16. Ensure your smile sheets measure factors that are aligned with science-of-learning recommendations, for example, the four pillars of training effectiveness: (1) understanding, (2) remembering, (3) motivation to apply, and (4) after-training supports.

17. Design your smile sheets as opportunities to send stealth messages—messages that hint at good learning-design practices.

# CHAPTER 5

## SMILE-SHEET QUESTION QUIZ

OKAY, DEAR READER, it's time to see if you can distinguish a good smile-sheet question from a bad one. This chapter consists entirely of questions for you to critique—with my critical reflections of those questions. First, I'll present the questions. Then you'll analyze them and I'll give you feedback on each question.

| Question #1 |
| :--- |
| **I learned new knowledge and skills from this training.** |
| A. Strongly Disagree |
| B. Disagree |
| C. Slightly Disagree |
| D. Neutral |
| E. Slightly Agree |
| F. Agree |
| G. Strongly Agree |

**Questions for You (the Reader) to Answer Now:**

Is this question reasonably well designed to be included on a smile sheet?

Circle: YES or NO

What is good about it?




What is bad about it?




Yo, reader! What the heck are you doing? You have to write down your responses. Really! There's good research that shows that if you take this kind of exercise seriously, you'll think more deeply about the issues, you'll learn more, and you'll remember what you learned for a longer period of time.

I know. You don't want to scar this beatific book. But truly, you will scar it by not writing in it.

### Feedback on Question #1

This question is terrible!

First, it uses a Likert-like scale, making it hard for learners to calibrate their answers and hard for stakeholders to understand the meaning of the outcomes reported.

Second, the statement, because it is conveyed as an affirmation, is likely to bias results toward positive outcomes.

But here is the most telling thing about Question 1. It is used and has been recommended for use by one of our industry's most popular learning-measurement consultancies. Seriously! Many of our learning-measurement "experts" simply don't know what they're doing.

| Question #2 |
| --- |
| **The training will have a significant impact on (check all that apply):** |
| A. Increasing Quality<br><br>B. Decreasing Costs<br><br>C. Decreasing Cycle Time<br><br>D. Increasing Productivity<br><br>E. Increasing Sales<br><br>F. Decreasing Risk<br><br>G. Increasing Employee Satisfaction<br><br>H. Increasing Customer Satisfaction |

**Questions for You (the Reader) to Answer Now:**

Is this question reasonably well designed to be included on a smile sheet?

Circle: YES or NO

What is good about it?

What is bad about it?

**Feedback on Question #2**

Wait. Wait. Wait. Do yourself a big favor and write down your answer first before reading this well-crafted feedback! And let me give you a hint. This question has both strengths and weaknesses. Go back and write down both the good and the bad.

Here's the feedback. Despite good points and bad, overall this question cannot be recommended.

First, what is good about it? Well, it uses descriptive answer choices (for example, "Increasing Quality"). This gives learners something specific to analyze. So that is one thing in its favor.

Unfortunately, there isn't much else going for this question. For example, all the choices are positive, severely biasing the results. This question begs for at least one of the answers to be chosen. When we report out on the data, there will then seem to be positive results, even though the data will reflect the question's influence, not the actual results.

In addition, we should ask whether our learners are good judges of whether these types of changes occur because of training. It seems doubtful that learners have accurate insights about whether a training program will decrease risk, increase customer satisfaction, and so forth.

I would not recommend this question for use on a smile sheet. Again, this question is taken directly from another of the top learning-measurement companies in our industry. That chief learning officers would fall for such an obviously biased question speaks to one of two things: either they just don't understand learning measurement or they want to look good regardless of the truth.

| **Question #3** |
| :---: |
| **In regard to the concepts taught in the course, how motivated will you be to utilize these skills in your work?** |
|   A.  I will NOT MAKE THIS A PRIORITY when I get back to my day-to-day job. <br><br>   B.  I will make this a PRIORITY—BUT A LOW PRIORITY— when I get back to my day-to-day job. <br><br>   C.  I will make this a MODERATE PRIORITY when I get back to my day-to-day job. <br><br>   D.  I will make this a HIGH PRIORITY when I get back to my day-to-day job. <br><br>   E.  I will make this one of my HIGHEST PRIORITIES when I get back to my day-to-day job. |

**Questions for You (the Reader) to Answer Now:**

Is this question reasonably well designed to be included on a smile sheet?

Circle: YES or NO

What is good about it?

What is bad about it?

## Feedback on Question #3

This question is a good one!

First, it directly focuses on one of the four pillars of training effectiveness, that is, whether learners are motivated to apply what they've learned.

Second, the answer choices give learners a choice between real alternatives—specifically, between different levels of priority they may have in applying the learning back on the job.

Finally, because of the way the answer choices are worded—and especially because of the capitalization of the key differentiators between the choices—when the results of this question are reported, it will be possible to highlight clear distinctions to stakeholders. Specifically, we will be able to report how many learners will make application of the learning a low priority, a moderate priority, a high priority, and so on.

---

| **Question #4** |
| :--- |
| **Using job aids or checklists can be an effective way to ensure you properly apply skills to your job. Which of the following are true? Circle as many items as are true.** |
| A.  We did NOT RECEIVE ANY WORTHWHILE job aids, checklists, or similar reminders to direct our on-the-job actions. <br><br> B.  We RECEIVED ONE OR MORE WORTHWHILE job aids, checklists, or similar prompting mechanisms. <br><br> C.  During the course, we USED ONE OR MORE WORTHWHILE job aids, checklists, or similar prompting mechanisms in REALISTIC PRACTICE EXERCISES. <br><br> D.  Between sessions of our course, IN OUR WORKSITES, WE UTILIZED one or more WORTHWHILE job aids, checklists, or similar prompting mechanisms IN A REAL-WORLD JOB TASK. |

**Questions for You (the Reader) to Answer Now:**

Is this question reasonably well designed to be included on a smile sheet?

Circle: YES or NO


What is good about it?




What is bad about it?




**Feedback on Question #4**

This question is a good one, although it can seem a little awkward for those of us accustomed to traditional smile sheets.

First, it focuses on one of the four pillars of training effectiveness, that is, whether there are after-training supports in place. Indeed, job aids provide great benefits in support of actual on-the-job performance. They are even more potent in supporting remembering when they are utilized within a training program.

Second, the answer choices give learners a choice between real alternatives, specifically, between qualitatively different levels of job-aid use; levels that are based on research.

Third—and also because the answer choices provide clear alternatives—this question can be reported out to stakeholders with enough clarity to drive action (the stealth messaging idea).

| Question #5 |
| --- |
| **Overall, how satisfied are you with this learning experience?** |
| A. Not at all satisfied. |
| B. Not very satisfied. |
| C. Somewhat satisfied. |
| D. Very satisfied. |
| E. Extremely satisfied. |

**Questions for You (the Reader) to Answer Now:**

Is this question reasonably well designed to be included on a smile sheet?

Circle: YES or NO

What is good about it?

What is bad about it?

**Feedback on Question #5**

This question is a poor one.

First, it focuses on learner satisfaction, which is not one of the essential factors in learning effectiveness. Remember, traditional smile sheets that use questions regarding learner satisfaction have not been correlated with learning results.

Second, while it doesn't use a full-bore Likert-like scale, the distinctions between the different levels of satisfaction still may be difficult for the learners to differentiate. Certainly, "extremely satisfied" is more descriptive than "strongly agree," but even more concreteness would be beneficial. Moreover, if we think ahead to how the answers will be reported out—and what the standards might be—it is unclear where the dividing line between acceptable and unacceptable levels of satisfaction would lie.

The question is also not actionable. Even if you learn that people aren't satisfied with the learning experience, the question doesn't tell you what's wrong.

To reiterate, the big problem with this question is that it is focused not on a primary goal of smile sheets (like training effectiveness), not a secondary goal (like learner understanding), and not even a tertiary goal (like whether the learners were engaged and attentive to the learning). It is focused on learner satisfaction, which is a fourth-level goal—far removed from whether the training is effective or not.

| Question #6 |
| --- |
| **How likely is it that you would recommend this training course to a friend or colleague?** |
| A. NOT AT ALL LIKELY to recommend |
| B. VERY UNLIKELY to recommend |
| C. SOMEWHAT UNLIKELY to recommend |
| D. SOMEWHAT LIKELY to recommend |
| E. VERY LIKELY to recommend |
| F. EXTREMELY LIKELY to recommend |

**Questions for You (the Reader) to Answer Now:**

Is this question reasonably well designed to be included on a smile sheet?

Circle: YES or NO

What is good about it?

What is bad about it?

## Feedback on Question #6

This question is also a poor one. Many organizations are beginning to utilize this type of question after having learned about the Net Promoter Score used in marketing. Unfortunately, there are many reasons to avoid using this type of question. See the blog post "Net Promoter Score: Maybe Fine for Marketing, Stupid for Training" to learn more. It's available on the web at www. is.gd/NetPromoterBad (use the caps!).

This question does not focus on any of the most important factors that relate to training effectiveness. As stated earlier, learners don't always know what makes good learning, so their recommendations are not likely to be related to training effectiveness. This is the key thing that is wrong with this question.

It can be argued that asking for this type of customer satisfaction data helps us determine whether our training course is meeting the expectations of an important stakeholder constituent—our learners. This does seem reasonable on the face of it, but since we've seen that such satisfaction data is uncorrelated with learning results, shouldn't we do more than to encourage these inappropriate expectations? Shouldn't we nudge our learners to expect more from their time and effort? Why can't we threshold their expectations to the level of improved on-the-job performance?

If you absolutely have to use the Net Promoter question—or a variant—make it one of the last questions after you've set the right level of expectations with better earlier questions.

# CHAPTER 6

## CANDIDATE QUESTIONS FOR A PERFORMANCE-FOCUSED SMILE SHEET

HOPEFULLY MOST OF THE ARGUMENTS I've made now resonate with you—and we can agree that smile sheets should target training effectiveness and actionable results. I, of course, will leave open the possibility that you have some quibbles—and that's okay; it's important that we all think for ourselves. Still, I'm guessing that I've been at least somewhat persuasive if you're still reading. No matter, it's time to look at candidate questions you might consider for your smile sheets.

Let me reiterate a key point. There are no perfect learning-measurement instruments, nor are there any perfect smile-sheet questions. Every word added or subtracted from a question implies trade-offs and a change in meaning. People will read questions differently. We are not creating exactitude. Instead, our aim is to be as true and as effective as possible and to always look for improvements. I've been working to improve my own smile sheets for years and years, and I'm sure I will continue seeing improvements I can make.

I'm going to offer some damn good questions here, but certainly you may see improvements you could make, for example, better ways to phrase something for your audience and your content areas. That's great! I highly recommend that you use the candidate questions based on your own wisdom and that you modify them when you think you can improve them. Of course, you might want to get other folks' feedback as well.

## Indexing Smile-Sheet Questions with the Smile-Sheet Training-Effectiveness Taxonomy

The questions will be indexed based on what we might call the smile-sheet training-effectiveness taxonomy, based partially on the four pillars of training effectiveness. More simply, this is a reiteration of the training-effectiveness goal structure I presented previously.

**Smile-Sheet Training-Effectiveness Taxonomy**

Smile-Sheet Primary Goal—Training Effectiveness

   Secondary Goal—Understanding

      Tertiary Goal—Learners Engaged

         Quaternary Goal*—Learners Motivated to Learn

         Quaternary Goal*—Instructors Credible and Engaging

         Quaternary Goal*—Environment Conducive to Learning

      Tertiary Goal—Cognitive Supports Effective

         Quaternary Goal*—Course Well-Organized

         Quaternary Goal*—Materials Signal Attention Hot Spots

         Quaternary Goal*—New Content Aligned to Prior Knowledge

   Secondary Goal—Remembering

      Tertiary Goal—Realistic Retrieval Practice

      Tertiary Goal—Spaced Repetitions

      Tertiary Goal—Situation-Action Triggering

Secondary Goal—Motivation to Apply

Tertiary Goal—Belief in Value of Concepts

Tertiary Goal—Self-Efficacy

Tertiary Goal—Resilience

Secondary Goal—After-Training Follow-Through

Tertiary Goal—Reminding Mechanisms

Tertiary Goal—Job Aids

Tertiary Goal—Supervisor Follow-Up

* Quaternary goals are included for completeness, but generally you won't want to create smile-sheet questions for them because they are at too low a priority for inclusion.

Ideally, each of the primary, secondary, and tertiary goals would have at least one question that examines how well the course targets it. Of course, if your smile sheet had one question for each of these goals, you would likely have too many questions to maintain your learners' attention and interest. Quaternary goals—those at the fourth level of priority—are included in the taxonomy too, but please note that these goals are a low-priority for smile-sheet questions because they are far removed from the primary goal.

The rest of this chapter introduces candidate questions indexed to the taxonomy above.

## Smile-Sheet Primary Goal—Training Effectiveness

Our primary goal in performance-focused training is to create improved on-the-job performance. Given that, we can ask our learners whether they feel they will be able to utilize the training concepts on the job.

Indeed, the following question is so good that I've been calling it the World's Best Smile-Sheet Question:

**Question 101**

**In regard to the course topics taught, HOW ABLE ARE YOU to put what you've learned into practice on the job?**

    A.  I'm NOT AT ALL ABLE to put the concepts into practice.

    B.  I have GENERAL AWARENESS of the concepts taught, but I will need more training / practice / guidance / experience TO DO ACTUAL JOB TASKS using the concepts taught.

    C.  I am ABLE TO WORK ON ACTUAL JOB TASKS, but I'LL NEED MORE HANDS-ON EXPERIENCE to be fully competent in using the concepts taught.

    D.  I am ABLE TO PERFORM ACTUAL JOB TASKS at a FULLY COMPETENT LEVEL in using the concepts taught.

    E.  I am ABLE TO PERFORM ACTUAL JOB TASKS at an EXPERT LEVEL in using the concepts taught.

The question is aimed specifically at training effectiveness. It asks learners for their impression of their ability to put the training concepts into practice on the job. This question is written so that in addition to being relevant at the end of training, it can also be deployed on a delayed smile sheet given to learners two to four weeks after the end of training.

Given that each question should be written with standards for acceptable results, here's my list of proposed standards for this question:

| Answer Choice | Proposed Standard |
|---|---|
| A. I'm NOT AT ALL ABLE to put the concepts into practice. | Unacceptable. |
| B. I have GENERAL AWARENESS of the concepts taught, but I WILL NEED MORE TRAINING / PRACTICE / GUIDANCE / EXPERIENCE TO DO ACTUAL JOB TASKS using the concepts taught. | For performance training: Unacceptable.<br><br>For awareness training: Acceptable. |
| C. I am ABLE TO WORK ON ACTUAL JOB TASKS, but I'LL NEED MORE HANDS-ON EXPERIENCE to be fully competent in using the concepts taught. | Acceptable. |
| D. I am ABLE TO PERFORM ACTUAL JOB TASKS at a FULLY COMPETENT LEVEL in using the concepts taught. | Superior Result. |
| E. I am ABLE TO PERFORM ACTUAL JOB TASKS at an EXPERT LEVEL in using the concepts taught. | Unlikely Result unless this training serves learners who are experts. |

This question's inherent message—one designed to reverberate as a stealth message—is that the focus of training is on-the-job performance. In addition, the question makes a distinction between awareness training and performance training—not by naming them, but in the difference between choice B, which shows the training creating "general awareness," and choice C, which indicates the training has created a minimal level of job skills.

Note my suggestions for standards should be seen as somewhat flexible given the type of course that is being taught. For example, a course that teaches conflict-resolution skills might warrant a different set of standards than a course teaching how to use a piece of software.

Other questions could also target on-the-job performance, the highest level of the taxonomy. For example:

---

**Question 102**

**Select the answer that best describes what the course enabled you to do, if anything.**

A. It DID NOT enable me to UNDERSTAND NEW CONCEPTS or USE NEW SKILLS.

B. It enabled me to UNDERSTAND SOME NEW CONCEPTS, but did NOT PREPARE ME TO USE NEW SKILLS on the job.

C. It enabled me to BEGIN TRYING TO USE NEW SKILLS on the job.

D. It enabled me to CONFIDENTLY USE NEW SKILLS on the job.

E. It enabled me to BE THOROUGHLY CONFIDENT AND PRACTICED IN USING NEW SKILLS on the job.

F. It enabled me to ACT LIKE AN EXPERT IN APPLYING NEW SKILLS on the job.

---

Note that both of the questions presented in this section (Questions 101 and 102) have as the most desirable choice an option that will almost always be unrealistic to achieve. The question above says that the training "enabled me to ACT LIKE AN EXPERT IN APPLYING NEW SKILLS on the job," a very unlikely occurrence. Adding these unrealistic options helps to slow down respondents so that they think critically about the answer choices. Given the tendency of smile-sheet respondents to circle the best answer without giving the answer choices much thought, this tactic may help limit people's ingrained uncritical responses. Of course, you'll need to show some wisdom about your organizational culture. Some organizational cultures—usually highly dysfunctional ones—expect to achieve the highest "grades" on everything. The expert answer choice may not work as intended in these contexts.

Note also that both of these questions—which target training effectiveness—also partially cover the secondary goal of learner understanding, at least in their "B" answer choices. In the question above, choice B asks whether the training enabled the respondent to understand some new concepts. But beware! Just because a question partially covers another goal, doesn't mean that it fully covers it. Indeed, without a question that specifically targets understanding, we haven't really covered understanding. We need to provide a question that gives learners options with different levels of understanding—as we will see in the next section. If we don't have different levels, we don't have the granularity that enables accurate decision making.

Here's one more example of a question that directly targets training effectiveness:

---

**Question 103**

**From your perspective, how valuable are the concepts taught in the course? HOW MUCH WILL THEY HELP YOU IMPROVE YOUR WORK OUTCOMES?**

   A.  Will NOT HELP ME to improve my work outcomes.

   B.  Will HELP ME SLIGHTLY to improve my work outcomes.

   C.  Will HELP ME A MODERATE AMOUNT to improve my work outcomes.

   D.  Will HELP ME SIGNIFICANTLY to improve my work outcomes.

   E.  Concepts taught are NOT RELEVANT to my work.

---

This question is not as good as the World's Best Smile-Sheet Question because its answer choices are not as descriptive. Indeed, these choices are similar to Likert-like answer choices in that we are asking learners to calibrate using fuzzy words like "slightly," "moderate," and "significantly." Of course, we should remember that perfection is not necessary or likely—we are always dealing with shades of acceptability. One question you can ask yourself to give you insight about a question's acceptability is whether you can clearly delineate standards for the answer choices. This question, in my mind, passes that test, but just barely. I can see choices A and B being unacceptable, C being acceptable, and D being superior—with choice E being another type of unacceptability.

## Secondary Goal #1—Understanding

We've looked at overall effectiveness. Now it's time to drill down on each of the four pillars of training effectiveness. The first is Understanding.

The best way to measure whether learners understand concepts is to test them on those concepts. Using smile-sheet questions is a weak proxy for full tests of understanding, but still it is worth assessing understanding on our smile sheets, first, if we aren't adequately measuring understanding in some other way, and second, so that our smile sheets are doing everything they can to measure this critical factor.

Another consideration, and one that is usually overlooked, is that ideally we should consider using good instructional-design practices to ensure that learners have maximum insight into their level of understanding. To generate such insight, shortly before learners complete our smile sheets, we should provide learners with exercises, conceptual questions, scenario-based decisions, simulations, or hands-on practice to help them gauge their understanding on key concepts or skills.

Questions such as the following can be utilized:

---

**Question 104**

**Now that you've taken the course, how well do you feel you understand the concepts taught in the course?**

A.  I have some significant CONFUSIONS AND/OR BLIND SPOTS.

B.  I have a BASIC FAMILIARITY with the concepts.

C.  I have a SOLID UNDERSTANDING of the concepts.

D.  I have a COMPREHENSIVE UNDERSTANDING of the concepts.

E.  I have an EXPERT-LEVEL UNDERSTANDING of the concepts.

---

This is a nice question because it very simply targets learner understanding—and it offers five graduated options for learners to choose from.

So that you have some sense of how you might put standards on the various answer choices, I've provided examples.

| Answer Choice | Proposed Standard |
|---|---|
| A. I have some significant CONFUSIONS AND/OR BLIND SPOTS. | Unacceptable. |
| B. I have a BASIC FAMILIARITY with the concepts. | For performance training: Unacceptable.<br><br>For awareness training: Acceptable. |
| C. I have a SOLID UNDERSTANDING of the concepts. | Acceptable. |
| D. I have a COMPREHENSIVE UNDERSTANDING of the concepts. | Superior Result. |
| E. I have an EXPERT-LEVEL UNDERSTANDING of the concepts. | Unlikely Result unless this training serves learners who are experts. |

Here is another example of a question that assesses understanding.

---

**Question 105**

**How well did the course prepare you to understand the concepts?**

**(Select all that apply)**

A. Concepts were CLEARLY PRESENTED.

B. Concepts were REPEATED TO AID CLARITY.

C. Concepts were REPEATED USING VARIOUS METHODS.

D. We were ASKED TO USE CONCEPTS TO ANSWER QUESTIONS.

E. We were ASKED TO USE CONCEPTS IN MAKING DECISIONS ABOUT REALISTIC SITUATIONS.

F. We were ASKED TO USE CONCEPTS IN A SIMULATED ENVIRONMENT.

G. We were ASKED TO USE CONCEPTS IN A REALISTIC HANDS-ON SITUATION.

H. We received HELPFUL FEEDBACK ON OUR EFFORTS TO USE CONCEPTS.

I. Concepts were NOT WELL PRESENTED.

J. Concepts were NOT GIVEN ENOUGH PRACTICE.

K. Concepts were NOT ENSURED BECAUSE FEEDBACK WAS ABSENT OR POORLY PROVIDED.

---

Note how this type of question—with a select-all-that-apply design—requires a different approach to standard setting.

| Answer Choice | Proposed Standard |
|---|---|
| A. Concepts were CLEARLY PRESENTED. | Expected Design Element. |

| | |
|---|---|
| B. Concepts were REPEATED TO AID CLARITY. | Expected Design Element. |
| C. Concepts were REPEATED USING VARIOUS METHODS. | Expected Design Element. |
| D. We were ASKED TO USE CONCEPTS TO ANSWER QUESTIONS. | Acceptable Design Element. |
| E. We were ASKED TO USE CONCEPTS IN MAKING DECISIONS ABOUT REALISTIC SITUATIONS. | Superior Design Element. |
| F. We were ASKED TO USE CONCEPTS IN A SIMULATED ENVIRONMENT. | Excellent Design Element. |
| G. We were ASKED TO USE CONCEPTS IN A REALISTIC HANDS-ON SITUATION. | Excellent Design Element. |
| H. We received HELPFUL FEEDBACK ON OUR EFFORTS TO USE CONCEPTS. | Expected Design Element. |
| I. Concepts were NOT WELL PRESENTED. | Red Flag. |
| J. Concepts were NOT GIVEN ENOUGH PRACTICE. | Red Flag. |
| K. Concepts were NOT ENSURED BECAUSE FEEDBACK WAS ABSENT OR POORLY PROVIDED. | Red Flag. |

Note also how the standard setting for each question can drive stealth messaging. Anyone who looks at the standards here will see that presenting concepts is insufficient, that some sort of active practice is important, that feedback is important, and that practice in more realistic situations is best of all. Indeed, that is one of the primary purposes of this type of question. Certainly if we observed the course ourselves—or we hired a learning consultant to evaluate our course design—it would be obvious whether these "supports for understanding" were in place or not. The benefit of putting this question on the smile sheet is twofold. First, it sends stealth messages to trainers, instructional designers, and other stakeholders. Second, it gives us continuing feedback on these supports for understanding, as compared to once-a-year reviews that require significant time and money.

Of course, there's no reason that these standards couldn't be used by course designers to design the learning intervention in the first place. However, my experience working in the industry for almost thirty years tells me that these kinds of design interventions often fade away with time. Integrating them into your smile sheets gives you another opportunity to create a sustainable practice. Initially they drive stakeholder learning. Over time they institutionalize effectiveness.

### Understanding—Tertiary Goal: Learners Engaged

I'm not convinced any other questions are needed to assess learner understanding. Specifically, tertiary goals seem less essential here than for some of the other secondary goals. Nevertheless, for completeness—and so you can decide for yourself—here is a question that attempts to get at learner engagement.

---

**Question 106**

**How engaging was the learning?**

    A.  I felt COMPLETELY UNENGAGED.

    B.  I was OFTEN UNENGAGED.

    C.  I was OFTEN ENGAGED, BUT OFTEN NOT ENGAGED.

    D.  I was MOSTLY ENGAGED.

    E.  I was ALMOST ALWAYS ENGAGED.

---

Standards for this question might have choices D and E as the only acceptable findings.

***Understanding—Learners Engaged—Quaternary Goal: Instructors Credible***
We could drill down on learner engagement to get to the quaternary level. You might do this if some factor needs special illumination in your situation. For some audiences the credibility of the instructors is critical. For example, many very experienced people will only take training seriously if the instructors immediately demonstrate the highest levels of credibility.

Given that research shows that human beings tend to evaluate others based on two dimensions, warmth (with a connotation of trust) and competence, we might want our questions about instructors to drill down on these aspects as well as the other learning-related competencies we would normally ask them about.[22]

---

**Question 107**

**Which of the following were true about your course instructor? Select all that apply.**

A. Was OFTEN UNCLEAR or DISORGANIZED.

B. Was OFTEN SOCIALLY AWKWARD OR INAPPROPRIATE.

C. Exhibited UNACCEPTABLE LACK OF KNOWLEDGE.

D. Exhibited LACK OF REAL-WORLD EXPERIENCE.

E. Generally PERFORMED COMPETENTLY AS A TRAINER.

F. Showed DEEP SUBJECT-MATTER KNOWLEDGE.

G. Demonstrated HIGH LEVELS OF REAL-WORLD EXPERIENCE.

H. MOTIVATED ME to ENGAGE DEEPLY IN THE LEARNING.

I. Is a PERSON I CAME TO TRUST.

---

22  Fiske, Cuddy, & Glick (2007).

The answer choices above have a brutally honest tone to them. This has the benefit of truth telling, but may be shocking in some organizational cultures. If you're worried, it might be worth doing a pilot test on a small group of learners before you roll this out to everyone. Alternatively, you might get a group of advocates together—some representing trainers and some representing learners—to write answer choices that both groups can buy into. Remember to have positive and negative attributes along both dimensions—warmth (trust) and competence. On the other hand, you might decide that the straightforward nature of the answer choices is just what's needed. Good instructors will exhibit the good behaviors and avoid the bad behaviors.

### *Understanding—Tertiary Goal: Cognitive Supports Effective*

Again, tertiary goals are generally less important than the higher-level goals, but sometimes they may have particular relevance. Cognitive supports are critical in helping learners build correct mental models of learning concepts. Interestingly, because learners are unlikely to know what "cognitive supports" are, it may be difficult to ask about them specifically; instead, quaternary goals may have to be targeted. For example, in evaluating a course on a complicated, non-intuitive software program, it might be especially helpful to drill down on whether the learners received sufficient delayed practice. Often, software learners can perform a task right after they learned it, but not after a delay. If the course doesn't give learners practice after a delay, then learners are not getting adequate practice. A question to get at whether such a cognitive support has been provided is presented here as an example.

**Question 108**

**Which of the following were true about the opportunities you were given to practice using the software? Select all that apply.**

A. We were given ALMOST NO PRACTICE.

B. We were given INADEQUATE AMOUNTS OF PRACTICE.

C. We were given TOO MUCH PRACTICE.

D. We DID NOT GET ENOUGH HELPFUL FEEDBACK WHEN WE WERE PRACTICING.

E. We were OFTEN ASKED TO PRACTICE SOMETHING RIGHT AFTER WE LEARNED IT.

F. We were OFTEN ASKED TO PRACTICE SOMETHING MORE THAN AN HOUR AFTER WE HAD LEARNED IT.

G. We were OFTEN ASKED TO PRACTICE SOMETHING AT LEAST A DAY AFTER WE HAD LEARNED IT.

H. We generally RECEIVED SUFFICIENT AND HELPFUL FEEDBACK AFTER WE HAD PRACTICED A TASK.

One interesting aside. Choice C above—"We were given TOO MUCH PRACTICE"— needs to have a special note in its declaration of standards. Often learners underestimate how much practice they need, so it could be that a high response rate on this reflects *not* a truism but an incorrect perspective. But note that it would *not* be okay to remove this answer choice from the question, because that would leave the question open to a positivity bias—one that the learners might be able to sniff out.

## Secondary Goal #2—Remembering

It's time to turn to the second secondary goal, Remembering. Here again, the best way to gauge remembering is to measure it directly with concept tests, scenario-based decision making, simulations, hands-on exercises, and so forth—and to measure it after a time delay. To reiterate, measuring these things during learning or immediately after learning can only measure understanding. To measure remembering, we must measure learning after a delay.

Again, dear reader, you might be asking, *"Dr. Willy Boy, why are we trying to measure remembering on a smile sheet when it is only a weak proxy for remembering?"* Great question! It's great to have such bright readers—and such familiar ones. Remembering is worth assessing on our smile sheets for two reasons. First, most of us are not going to measure remembering directly—it is sad to say—so it's useful to gauge remembering in some way. Second, because smile sheets send stealth messages—whether we intend those messages to be sent or not—it's helpful to send the message that remembering is a critical goal for learning design. Moreover, by drilling down to remembering's tertiary goals, we can send specific messages about the importance of providing realistic practice, spacing repetitions over time, and using situation-action triggering. These learning methods are usually underutilized, making it unlikely that our learners will remember what they've learned, so it's critical that we highlight these methods for our stakeholders.

If direct tests of remembering are best done after a delay, the principle also has relevance for smile sheets. Indeed, if we take a smile-sheet question designed to measure understanding, but we tweak it so that we can provide it after a delay, such a smile-sheet question can gauge remembering. Here's an example:

**Question 109**

**In the training you took several weeks ago, you learned about the following topics:**

- Topic 1
- Topic 2
- Topic 3
- Topic 4
- Topic 5
- Topic 6
- Topic 7
- Topic 8
- Topic 9

**Now that you've been back in the workplace for several weeks after taking the training, how well do you feel you understand the concepts that were taught in the course?**

A.  I have some significant CONFUSIONS AND/OR BLIND SPOTS.

B.  I have a BASIC FAMILIARITY with the concepts.

C.  I have a SOLID UNDERSTANDING of the concepts.

D.  I have a COMPREHENSIVE UNDERSTANDING of the concepts.

E.  I have an EXPERT-LEVEL UNDERSTANDING of the concepts.

One thing about a delayed smile sheet is that it's critical to remind learners of the topics they learned. You could list the topics before the learners answer smile-sheet questions, as I did in the question above. Conversely, before you unveil the delayed smile sheet, you could give them a short booster session, give them a short quiz, provide them with scenario-based decisions, or use another means of reminding. Of course, if you're going to go to all that trouble, you'll probably get a better measure of remembering from testing their knowledge and skills directly.

You could also ask people more directly about each topic, as in the following question.

---

**Question 110**

**Here is a topic you learned about:**

**Topic 1 details would be inserted here . . .**

**How well do you remember the concepts and skills related to Topic 1?**

    A.  I remembered ALMOST NOTHING about this topic.

    B.  I remember VERY LITTLE about this topic.

    C.  I remember SOME DETAILS about this topic.

    D.  I remember a SUBSTANTIAL AMOUNT about this topic.

    E.  I remember ALMOST EVERYTHING about this topic.


**Here is another topic you learned about:**

**Topic 2 details would be inserted here . . .**

**How well do you remember the concepts and skills related to Topic 2?**

    A.  I remembered ALMOST NOTHING about this topic.

    B.  I remember VERY LITTLE about this topic.

    C.  I remember SOME DETAILS about this topic.

    D.  I remember a SUBSTANTIAL AMOUNT about this topic.

    E.  I remember ALMOST EVERYTHING about this topic.

---

I offer the questions above more as thought exercises than as a set of recommended questions. If you were going to have a specific question for each topic, you'd be better off creating a nicely designed scenario-based question to test people's memory directly.

Indeed, asking learners how much they remember is a poor smile-sheet question. Certainly, asking them how much they think they'll remember is not going to capture good data. Therefore, one of the key points is that in measuring remembering on smile sheets, we are better off looking at the tertiary goals.

### *Remembering's Tertiary Goals*

- Realistic Retrieval Practice

- Spaced Repetitions

- Situation-Action Triggering

We will now look at each of these in turn.

### *Remembering—Tertiary Goal: Realistic Retrieval Practice*

One of the best ways to support our learners in remembering is to provide them with realistic practice, prompting them to retrieve concepts from memory and, specifically, prompting them to retrieve information in a manner that is similar to that which they will face on the job. I am specifically *not* talking about retrieving low-level, trivial information. As Shrock and Coscarelli (2007) warned us, memorization questions are not acceptable proxies for real-world performance. Realistic practice entails providing learners with realistic background situations and having them make decisions and/or practice skills.

Here's a question that gauges the level of realistic practice given in a training course.

---

**Question 111**

**HOW MUCH OF THE TRAINING WAS DEVOTED TO GIVING YOU PRACTICE working on real job tasks or giving you realistic simulations, scenarios, or exercises related to real job tasks?**

A. 0% of the training was devoted to realistic practice.

B. 10%

C. 20%

D. 30%

E. 40%

F. 50% of the training was devoted to realistic practice.

G. 60%

H. 70%

I. 80%

J. 90%

K. 100% of the training was devoted to realistic practice.

---

I've chosen to give people answer choices at 10% intervals from 0% to 100%. I've done this because my gut tells me that people are better able to calibrate their decision making if they can see a range of responses but not too many responses—but I'm not sure about this, and haven't seen any empirical evidence one way or another. Nevertheless, providing my eleven-item range, instead of using 0–20%, 20%–40%, and so on, or less than 35%, 35%–60%, and so on, seems to me to have another advantage—the advantage of always asking the learners the same question—to enable comparison between different courses. In this way, the question is the same, but the standards for acceptable levels of realistic retrieval practice vary for different types of courses. For example, for a performance training leadership-development course, the acceptable range might be 40% to 70%, whereas for a writing course, the acceptable range might be 60% to 90% (that is, 60% to 90% of the course should provide realistic retrieval practice).

Let me say this: For any course that aspires to be a performance training course—one devoted to actually producing on-the-job benefits—the absolute minimum percentage of the course devoted to realistic practice should be 35%. Absolute minimum! Most of us—me included—forget this, and try to cram too much content into our training courses. Providing realistic practice in significant amounts is not a luxury; it's a requirement.

Another way to gauge realistic practice is to ask about the specific types of practice that we could offer our learners.

---

**Question 112**

**Which types of practice were you given in this training course? Select all that apply.**

    A.  We were NOT given any practice opportunities.

    B.  Quiz-like questions on our knowledge of basic terminology and basic concepts—on information not necessarily needed for successful job performance.

    C.  Quiz-like questions on our knowledge of terminology and concepts critical to actual job performance.

    D.  Short, realistic job-related scenarios followed by questions.

    E.  Longer job-related case studies followed by questions.

    F.  Short exercises on realistic job tasks.

    G.  Extensive exercises on realistic job tasks.

    H.  Simulations of realistic job tasks.

    I.  Real job tasks.

---

The standards for this question would state that choices A and B are inadequate; choice C is acceptable; and the rest of the choices are superior.

### *Remembering—Tertiary Goal: Spaced Repetitions*

The spacing effect is the finding that spacing repetitions over time provides more effective support for long-term remembering than repeating things without a delay or with a shorter delay.[23] Spaced repetitions of two weeks are likely to produce better remembering than spaced repetitions of one week. One day is better than half a day. Two hours is better than one hour. Fifteen minutes is better than five minutes. As Harry Bahrick and Linda Hall once noted in a top-tier scientific journal, the *Journal of Memory and Language*, "The spacing effect is one of the oldest and best documented phenomena in the history of learning and memory research."[24] It is interesting that the spacing effect was, until recently, one of the most underutilized key learning factors in the training-and-development field.

To gauge a training program's utilization of the spacing effect, we might use the following question.

---

23   Scientific reviews of the spacing literature: Carpenter, Cepeda, Rohrer, Kang, & Pashler (2012); Delaney, Verkoeijen, & Spirgel (2010); Thalheimer (2006); Donovan & Radosevich (1999); Lee & Genovese (1988); Ruch (1928); Cain & Willey (1939); Melton (1970); Crowder (1976); Hintzman (1974); Glenberg (1979); Rea & Modigliani (1988); Dempster (1988, 1989, 1996).

24   Bahrick & Hall (2005).

**Question 113**

**Which of the following are true about the scheduling of topics in this course? Select as many as are true.**

A. We covered each topic once, NEVER OR RARELY RETURNING TO A TOPIC AFTER IT WAS COVERED.

B. For many topics covered, we put the topics aside for AT LEAST AN HOUR and CAME BACK TO THE SAME TOPICS LATER AFTER COVERING OTHER TOPICS.

C. For many topics covered, we put the topics aside AT LEAST UNTIL THE NEXT DAY and CAME BACK TO THE SAME TOPICS LATER AFTER COVERING OTHER TOPICS.

D. For many topics covered, we put the topics aside, WENT BACK TO OUR WORKSITES to do our regular work, and CAME BACK TO THE SAME TOPICS AFTER WAITING AT LEAST UNTIL THE NEXT DAY.

E. For many topics covered, we put the topics aside, WENT BACK TO OUR WORKSITES to do our regular work, and CAME BACK TO THE SAME TOPICS AFTER WAITING AT LEAST A WEEK.

| Answer Choice | Proposed Standard |
|---|---|
| A. We covered each topic once, NEVER OR RARELY RETURNING TO A TOPIC AFTER IT WAS COVERED. | Unacceptable. |
| B. For many topics covered, we put the topics aside for AT LEAST AN HOUR and CAME BACK TO THE SAME TOPICS LATER AFTER COVERING OTHER TOPICS. | Acceptable only for short courses of less than about 8 hours' duration—unless longer spaced repetitions are used as well to augment these spacings. |

| C. For many topics covered, we put the topics aside AT LEAST UNTIL THE NEXT DAY and CAME BACK TO THE SAME TOPICS LATER AFTER COVERING OTHER TOPICS. | Acceptable. |
|---|---|
| D. For many topics covered, we put the topics aside, WENT BACK TO OUR WORKSITES to do our regular work, and CAME BACK TO THE SAME TOPICS AFTER WAITING AT LEAST UNTIL THE NEXT DAY. | Superior Result. |
| E. For many topics covered, we put the topics aside, WENT BACK TO OUR WORKSITES to do our regular work, and CAME BACK TO THE SAME TOPICS AFTER WAITING AT LEAST A WEEK. | Excellent Result. |

Note that the granularity in the answer choices could be increased even further by adding the following options, which might be desirable if we are evaluating shorter courses:

- For many topics covered, we put the topics aside for AT LEAST HALF AN HOUR and CAME BACK TO THE SAME TOPICS LATER AFTER COVERING OTHER TOPICS.
- For many topics covered, we put the topics aside for AT LEAST TWO HOURS and CAME BACK TO THE SAME TOPICS LATER AFTER COVERING OTHER TOPICS.

Indeed, we could add answer choices to get at micro-spacings—spacings of less than a few minutes—which is a learning design that is often appropriate for intense applications like language learning.

However, the question as written does a nice job sending very clear stealth messages about what is really desirable in terms of spaced repetitions. Short spacings are good. Spacings over a day are better. Spacings over a longer time frame are even better. By being very clear about the benefits of longer spacings, we may get our stakeholders onboard with more effective learning designs, including such things as subscription learning applications.

### *Remembering—Tertiary Goal: Situation-Action Triggers*

Situation-action triggers have been shown—in extensive scientific refereed research—to be extremely effective in helping people remember what to do in future situations.[25] Essentially, if we can get people to link situations with actions they plan to take, they'll be much more likely to remember what they were planning to do than if such a link was never made.

There are several prominent learning methods that parlay this scientific fact. One is triggered action planning. Action planning is well known. It occurs at the end of training when we ask learners what goals they have for taking what they've learned back to the job. Triggered action planning makes action planning much more likely to actually be followed through. In triggered action planning learners are not only asked what goals they have for learning implementation, but they're asked to think about the situations in which their goals will be realized. For example, in a leadership course, a learner might have the goal of bringing his or her direct reports into decision making. To use triggered action planning, a person might decide that the situation to target is an upcoming staff meeting, and the action to target is asking for input into a particular decision. This situation-action pair becomes the engine for triggered action planning—with the expectation that when the learner encounters the situation (the staff meeting or the planning for it), he or she will be much more likely to remember to ask his or her direct reports to participate in the decision making.

A second way to utilize situation-action triggering is to prepare learners with intense practice to deal with various contingencies—to plan and practice

---

25  Gollwitzer & Sheeran (2006).

specific actions, each aimed at one of multiple situations. A similar methodology can be used specifically to help learners deal with obstacles or problems they might be expected to face on the job. This situation-action type of "inoculation" strategy plans for problem situations and pairs these with both actions and metacognitive strategies for how to deal with the potential emotional blowback from hitting the obstacle.

The bottom line on situation-action triggering is that we are using the natural human tendency to be reactive to stimuli as a way to prepare our learners to respond appropriately when they encounter certain on-the-job stimuli.

Of course, our learners are not going to understand the science or terminology behind this, so writing a smile-sheet question is going to be a bit tricky. Here's a question I've come up with.

**Question 114**

**One training method that has been found to be particularly effective in helping learners like yourself prepare for on-the-job situations is to have you plan or practice what you'll do in future on-the-job situations so that you have a ready plan of action for various targeted situations.**

**How many of the following methods did you experience in this training? Select all that apply.**

A.  We did action planning where we (1) first determined what goals we wanted to accomplish on the job in using what we learned in training, (2) decided what key situations we would target for each goal, and (3) came up with a plan of action for each of those key situations.

B.  We intensively practiced making decisions and/or taking actions in numerous practical job-related situations, developing a clear plan of action for each of the situations.

C.  We planned for and practiced the actions we would take if later on the job we encountered certain difficult or problematic situations, and we prepared ourselves mentally for dealing with those obstacles and difficulties.

D.  We talked about how to deal with numerous practical job-related situations, and though we didn't practice them extensively, we did develop clear plans of actions for each situation.

E.  We did not engage in any of the above methods, but we did talk in general about how to handle certain on-the-job situations.

F.  We did zero or very little planning or preparation for specific on-the-job situations.

As you can see from the answer choices, this question can send powerful stealth messages about what should be done with situation-action triggering.

In considering the standards for acceptable responses, choices A, B, and C are very potent uses of the scientific finding. Choice D is acceptable. Choice E is unacceptable, and choice F is obviously suboptimal.

### Secondary Goal #3—Motivation to Apply

Learners who don't leave training with a large dose of motivation to apply what they've learned are learners who are unlikely to use what they've learned on the job. Certainly, they are unlikely to bring to bear the energy and metacognitive effort needed to circumnavigate obstacles, marshal resources, and persevere against the wave of normal on-the-job distractions.

Fortunately, measuring our learners' motivation is fairly straightforward. Here is a good question.

---

**Question 115**

**In regard to the concepts taught in the course, how motivated WILL YOU BE to UTILIZE these skills in your work?**

    A. I will NOT MAKE THIS A PRIORITY when I get back to my day-to-day job.

    B. I will make this a PRIORITY—BUT A LOW PRIORITY—when I get back to my day-to-day job.

    C. I will make this a MODERATE PRIORITY when I get back to my day-to-day job.

    D. I will make this a HIGH PRIORITY when I get back to my day-to-day job.

    E. I will make this one of my HIGHEST PRIORITIES when I get back to my day-to-day job.

---

In terms of standards, choices A and B are unacceptable, choice C is acceptable, and choices D and E are superior.

In addition to targeting Motivation to Apply directly—as in the above question—we can also target its tertiary goals.

### *Motivation-to-Apply's Tertiary Goals*

- Belief in the Value of Concepts

- Self-Efficacy

- Resilience

We will now look at each of these in turn.

### *Motivation to Apply—Tertiary Goal: Belief in the Value of Concepts*

Although we as learning professionals might not like to admit it, learners may not always believe in the concepts we teach them. While this is more likely to be an issue in soft skills training, it can even be true for technical training. I'll never forget sitting in the back of a diversity-training program watching a participant who simply believed that his black colleagues were inferior and that he had every right to treat them as inferiors. Startling, yes!—but a worst-case example of how learners might not believe what we are teaching them. Generally, when people don't believe in the value of the concepts taught, they play along and we don't notice their objections.

We'd be fooling ourselves if we didn't think that beliefs weren't critical to people's motivation. Would you be motivated to put ideas into practice that you didn't believe in? I think not!

Here's a question that can help you assess the strength of people's belief in the concepts taught.

---

**Question 116**

**The following five principles provided the basis for this training course.**

- Principle 1...
- Principle 2...
- Principle 3...
- Principle 4...
- Principle 5...

**You may believe in these deeply, or not at all. Rate each one on its importance to you.**

A. I BELIEVE DEEPLY in this principle.

B. I BELIEVE in this principle.

C. I CAN ACCEPT this principle.

D. I DO NOT ACCEPT this principle.

E. I BELIEVE DEEPLY that this principle IS FLAWED.

---

Note that this question—because it asks learners to respond to each principle separately—will require a more advanced question type than a simple multiple-choice format. Fortunately, most good survey software can implement this kind of question easily. If you're using paper-and-pencil smile sheets, you can create a grid with the principles down the left side and the answer choices represented in columns. Standards of acceptability for the question above might have choices A and B being acceptable and choices C, D, and E being unacceptable. It is not enough that people accept a principle. Our job as trainers is to help our learners believe deeply in the principles we teach.

### *Motivation to Apply—Tertiary Goal—Self-Efficacy*

People's motivations are also tied to their sense of self-efficacy about whether they can implement what they want to implement. This is not a generalized sense of self-efficacy, but a self-efficacy tied to specific job skills.

Here's a question to measure self-efficacy.

---

**Question 117**

**This training course was designed to teach you skills that you can use on the job. How confident do you feel that you can competently put these skills into practice?**

    A. I AM EXTREMELY CONFIDENT that I can successfully use these skills.

    B. I AM CONFIDENT that I can successfully use these skills.

    C. I AM PARTIALLY CONFIDENT that I can successfully use these skills.

    D. I AM NOT VERY CONFIDENT that I can successfully use these skills.

    E. I HAVE ZERO CONFIDENCE that I can successfully use these skills.

---

The standards of acceptable responses for this question would probably vary depending on the difficulty of the content taught. However, as a general rule, choices A and B would be acceptable, and choices C, D, and E would be unacceptable.

But beware! Beware! Questions of this type—asking about a person's confidence in their own ability—are likely to suffer from extreme bias. Why? Because people are not always good at knowing what they're able to do—especially if they haven't been given true tests of their ability.

I remember, as a young man, thinking that I might have been a good baseball player if only I had started playing organized baseball earlier. One of the guys on my high school baseball team told me that although I was the best softball player in our high school, he was a better baseball player. In my mind, I had talent but not enough baseball experience. These delusions of my youthful potential as a star baseball player were fueled by the fact that my skills had never been tested. Being good at stick ball and softball, it turns out, aren't an adequate test of one's baseball skills. Indeed, when several years later I found that I could only throw a baseball at 47 miles per hour, when the average big leaguer easily threw over 80 miles per hour, I finally realized that my childhood beliefs in my baseball self-efficacy had been a warm-wash-of-summertime delusion.

Here's the tricky part about measuring self-efficacy and confidence as they relate to training. A training course that really challenges people in attempting new skills is actually less likely to prompt high ratings of self-efficacy than a course that gives minimal challenge—and thus minimal preparation. This is one reason why awareness training is so popular even though it doesn't do very much to prepare learners for real on-the-job performance. Awareness training prompts people to believe in their own self-efficacy—even when they are not very skilled.

Are there better ways to measure self-efficacy than the question above? Perhaps; I'm not sure. Certainly, the question above might provide valid data if learners had previously been challenged with realistic job-related tasks. But based on the question alone, we would have no way of knowing whether such challenges had been offered. If authentic challenges were offered by one instructor and not another, the question would likely produce biased results.

We are left with the question, is there a way to measure self-efficacy that doesn't suffer from this inherent human bias? Here's my best attempt.

---

**Question 118**

**How prepared are you to apply skills from this training to real work situations? Select as many as are true.**

    A.  I AM CONFIDENT that I can successfully use these skills, because between the start and end of training I ACTUALLY USED THESE SKILLS IN DOING REAL WORK.

    B.  I AM CONFIDENT that I can successfully use these skills, because the TRAINING CHALLENGED ME MANY TIMES WITH DIFFICULT JOB-RELATED TASKS.

    C.  I AM CONFIDENT that I can successfully use these skills, because the training provided me with PRACTICE ON REALISTIC JOB-RELATED TASKS.

    D.  I AM CONFIDENT that I can successfully use these skills, even though the training DID NOT PROVIDE MUCH PRACTICE ON REALISTIC JOB-RELATED TASKS.

    E.  I AM NOT VERY CONFIDENT that I can successfully use these skills.

    F.  I HAVE ZERO CONFIDENCE that I can successfully use these skills.

---

Given the challenge inherent in creating a question on self-efficacy, this is a pretty good attempt. Here's what I like about it. It shakes the learner into wakefulness. By hinting that there is a causal relationship between the amount of realistic challenge and one's competence level, learners are likely to be less cocksure of their own ability. Also, the question does a nice job of setting itself up to send valuable stealth messages. It specifically hints at the idea that real-world job challenges and extensive practice on difficult tasks help create skilled competence. Of course, the question alone won't make this statement without explicit standards of acceptable responses. Here choices A and B are superior, choice C is borderline acceptable, and choices D, E, and F are unacceptable.

### *Motivation to Apply—Tertiary Goal—Resilience*

Resilience is characteristic of people who will persevere in constructive efforts even when they face difficulties, obstacles, and misfortunes. While the traditional connotation of resilience involves a general long-term state of being, for our purposes, it's more helpful to see resilience as context specific. Indeed, a person might be resilient in applying one type of training to their work and nonresilient in applying another type of training.

The following question is designed to measure a person's sense of their own resilience.

**Question 119**

**Sometimes people—people just like you—will face obstacles or difficulties when they attempt to apply new learning to their jobs. How prepared are you to overcome such difficulties in terms of applying the skills from this training course? Select all that apply.**

A. I WILL PERSEVERE IN THE FACE OF DIFFICULTIES to apply the learning, BECAUSE I BELIEVE STRONGLY in the importance of the content of this course.

B. I WILL PERSEVERE IN THE FACE OF DIFFICULTIES to apply the learning, BECAUSE THE TRAINING PREPARED ME FOR MANY OF THE DIFFICULT SITUATIONS I MIGHT FACE.

C. I WILL PERSEVERE IN THE FACE OF DIFFICULTIES to apply the learning, BECAUSE THE TRAINING PREPARED ME TO BE MENTALLY RESILIENT.

D. I WILL PERSEVERE IN THE FACE OF DIFFICULTIES to apply the learning, BECAUSE I HAVE COWORKERS WHO HAVE PLEDGED TO SUPPORT ME IN DOING THIS.

E. I WILL PERSEVERE IN THE FACE OF DIFFICULTIES to apply the learning, BECAUSE MY BOSS HAS PLEDGED TO PROVIDE GUIDANCE, SUPPORT, AND RESOURCES.

F. DESPITE NOT HAVING ANY OF THESE HELPFUL SUPPORTS, I AM LIKELY TO PERSEVERE IN THE FACE OF DIFFICULTIES to apply the learning.

G. I AM UNLIKELY TO PERSEVERE IN THE FACE OF DIFFICULTIES to apply the learning.

Note how this question uses the same strategy as the question immediately before it on self-efficacy. That is, it primes the respondent to think deeply about what causes—or what can influence—resilience. This design not only helps the learners make better decisions on this question, but it also sets up the question to send stealth messages about what is needed for learner resilience.

Standards for acceptable responses for this question are as follows: choices A, B, C, D, and E are acceptable responses. Choices F and G are unacceptable. Again, this question can be used to send the message that we as workplace learning-and-performance professionals—and our colleagues on the business side—can play key roles in supporting learners in being resilient.

Again, we must be cautious when asking human beings to comment on their own traits. Question 119 may simply be asking too much of learners. Indeed, two wicked-smart folks who reviewed an early version of this manuscript questioned whether learners would be good at assessing their own perseverance. I've left the question in the book to let you, the reader, decide, but also because I think it's good to emphasize again how critical it is to consider learner decision-making capability when we design our questions. One quick fix to question 119 is to simply ask the learners about the supports they received in the training.

---

**Question 119 – Version 2**

**Sometimes people—people just like you—will face obstacles or difficulties when they attempt to apply new learning to their jobs. What preparations did the course provide to help you deal with the obstacles you might face? Select all that apply!**

A. The training MOTIVATED ME TO BELIEVE STRONGLY in the importance of the concepts and skills taught in this course.

B. The training GAVE ME PRACTICE DEALING WITH MANY OF THE DIFFICULT SITUATIONS I MIGHT FACE in applying the learning.

C. The training gave me PRACTICE IN BEING MENTALLY RESILIENT IN THE FACE OF OBSTACLES.

D. The training prompted me to ENLIST COWORKERS TO PLEDGE TO SUPPORT ME in applying the learning.

E. The training helped ENLIST MY BOSS TO PROVIDE GUIDANCE, SUPPORT, AND RESOURCES.

F. The training did LITTLE OR NOTHING TO HELP ME FACE THE WORKPLACE OBTACLES I MAY FACE in applying the learning.

---

## Secondary Goal #4—After-Learning Follow-Through

The final of the four pillars is After-Learning Follow-Through. Like Remembering, it is difficult to measure directly on a smile sheet but will ideally be measured instead through its tertiary goals.

### *After-Learning Follow-Through's Tertiary Goals*

- Reminding Mechanisms

- Job Aids

- Supervisor Follow-Through

It is worth noting the obvious here—in case it's not obvious. These three tertiary goals are certainly not the only things we could measure in regard to after-learning follow-through. For example, we might want to measure whether learners are required to complete a work project, whether they have to report their results, or whether a training application goal-monitoring system is in place. You are certainly encouraged to create your own questions if they have particular relevance to your organization or training goals.

I'm going to focus on what I consider to be the three most important factors for successful after-learning follow-through. We will look at each of these in turn, but first, I'll convey a question that attempts to cover all of these considerations in one smile-sheet question.

**Question 120**

**After the course, when you begin to apply your new knowledge at your worksite, which of the following supports are likely to be in place for you?**

**Circle as many items as are likely to be true.**

A. I will have ENOUGH TIME to work on applying the learning.

B. I will be ENCOURAGED BY MY SUPERVISOR to apply the learning to real job tasks.

C. I will have my PROGRESS MONITORED BY MY SUPERVISOR in applying the learning.

D. I will have someone available TO COACH OR MENTOR ME in applying the learning.

E. I will have easy access to FELLOW LEARNERS to contact for guidance and support.

F. I will have easy access to a COURSE INSTRUCTOR to contact for guidance and support.

G. I will be ENCOURAGED BY MY COWORKERS to apply the learning to real job tasks.

H. I will have JOB AIDS to guide me in applying the learning to real job tasks.

I. I will be PERIODICALLY REMINDED of key learning concepts/ skills through some systematic after-learning intervention(s).

J. I will NOT get much direct support, but will rely on my own initiative.

While utilizing a single question here is more efficient than using three questions to get at all three tertiary goals, it is unlikely to be as effective as more-targeted questions. Perhaps even more important, it will not engender stealth messaging as clearly and strongly as separate questions would enable.

Also, there are so many answer choices above that some of your respondents may get glassy eyeballs and lose their ability to focus. While the question above may seem perfectly acceptable, when you look at the separate questions provided below, you'll see how much more clarity can be squeezed from these interactions. Of course, you will have to weigh precision against the downside of asking three questions instead of one.

The standards for acceptable responses for this question might have choices A to I being acceptable, and choice J being unacceptable.

We'll now turn to each of the After-Learning Follow-Through's tertiary goals, starting with reminding mechanisms.

### *After-Learning Follow-Through—Tertiary Goal—Reminding Mechanisms*

Learners benefit from reminders for three primary reasons. First, learners forget, and reminders help them to remember what they learned. Second, reminders keep learners' goals for applying the new concepts fresh in mind so that they are more likely to devote metacognitive planning and effort to learning application. Third, reminders can convey social pressure in terms of expected outcomes.

The following question is designed to measure whether reminding mechanisms are in place after learning events end.

**Question 121**

**We humans forget stuff. We even forget important concepts and skills we've learned in training. Being reminded can help us remember.**

**Given what you've been told by your trainers, your boss, or your other coworkers, how do you expect to be reminded after this training ends? Select all that apply.**

A. My fellow learners and I are enrolled (or will be enrolled) on an email list that will send periodic reminders regarding the key concepts and skills we learned.

B. The course instructor(s) will contact us many times after the training to share key concepts, encourage discussions, monitor our progress, help us handle our difficulties, and/or support us in applying what we learned.

C. My boss is planning to follow up with me to support me as I work to implement what we learned in my job.

D. My fellow learners and I have additional work-related projects to complete before we are officially done with the course.

E. I have already made a specific plan to do additional reading, review my notes, watch videos, listen to podcasts, work with a colleague, and/or remind myself in some other way.

F. At this time, I know of NO reminders that I will receive.

Question 121 will be especially relevant and valuable for training courses that are delivered long before the new information is actually needed. The longer the time between learning and application, the more forgetting will take place—and the more critical it will be to provide learners with reminders.

On the other hand, forgetting happens almost immediately regardless of the time delay between learning and application. Here's a thought experiment that will help to make this clear. Suppose you teach your learners thirty key points. How many of these will they use on their first day back on the job? Let's say they'll use five. How many in the first week? Let's say ten more. This means that your learners will have to remember—and keep fresh in mind—half of what they learned longer than a week. And what of the other fifteen learning points? Certainly, some of those points won't be needed in the first month after training. Won't they be forgotten without some sort of reminder? The bottom line here is that even when a training course is delivered just in time, much of what was learned will have to be remembered over a long period of time—and thus reminders become critical.

### *After-Learning Follow-Through—Tertiary Goal: Job Aids*

Fortunately, most of us recognize that remembering is not the only method to spur on-the-job performance. We can prompt behavior directly through job aids, checklists, performance support tools, and other prompting mechanisms.

If we take a step back for a moment and reflect on human cognition, we can see that all human behavior is engendered through working memory—and, there are two general conduits to working memory, remembering and prompting.[26] We, as human beings, can activate working memory by either retrieving information from long-term memory or by being prompted by external cues in our environment.

The Learning Landscape model—my way of diagramming the practical complexity of workplace learning—has this two-source working-memory conception at the heart of its structure. In the diagram that follows, I've highlighted this two-source (remembering and prompting) notion as the Working-Memory Trigger Zone.

---

26  Although this two-source working-memory model is a simplification of very complex cognitive phenomena, for our purposes as learning professionals it represents underlying truths that have significant practical implications.

## The Learning Landscape

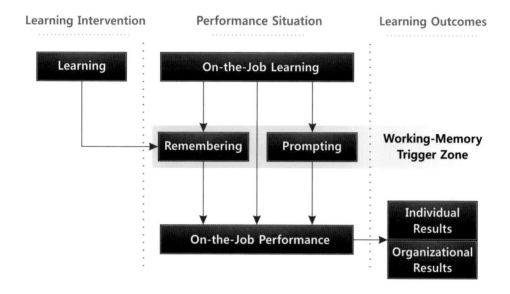

If you'd like to learn more about the Learning Landscape model, you can check out my YouTube video at http://is.gd/LearningLandscape.

Although there are many prompting mechanisms we could target in designing our smile sheets, I'm focusing mostly on job aids because these are the most popular prompting mechanisms—and the ones most likely to be used in conjunction with training programs.

Here is a question that we can use to measure the use of job aids in training.

**Question 122**

**Using job aids, checklists, or other prompting mechanisms can be an effective way to ensure you properly apply skills to your job. Which of the following are true?**

**Circle as many items as are true.**

A. We did NOT RECEIVE ANY WORTHWHILE job aids, checklists, or similar prompting mechanisms to direct our on-the-job actions.

B. We RECEIVED ONE OR MORE WORTHWHILE job aids, checklists, or similar prompting mechanisms.

C. During the course, we USED ONE OR MORE WORTHWHILE job aids, checklists, or similar prompting mechanisms in REALISTIC PRACTICE EXERCISES.

D. Between sessions of our course, IN OUR WORKSITES, WE UTILIZED one or more WORTHWHILE job aids, checklists, or similar prompting mechanisms IN A REAL-WORLD JOB TASK.

The standards for acceptable responses for this question might be as follows. Choice A is completely unacceptable. Choice B is also unacceptable— because unless a job aid is actually used in a training course, it is not likely to be used on the job. (Nor will it engender context-based remembering, but that's another story.) Choice C is acceptable. Choice D is superior. Note, of course, that job aids are not desirable for all learning-to-performance situations. Sometimes we want learners to internalize what they've learned and be able to perform without external prompting mechanisms.

It may seem odd to ask about whether job aids are used in a training course, since we are the ones providing the training. *"Holy Dr. Bobo Doll, couldn't we just answer this question ourselves?"* That's a great query, dear reader, but the answer may be surprising. Yes, we as learning professionals can certainly answer this question ourselves. However, there are several difficulties with this tactic. What's designed into a course isn't always what is utilized with learners. For example, we may have developed a great job aid, but during our course, when we find time running short, we may only mention the job aid in passing. Also, learners may not notice the use of a job aid if we don't effectively communicate it—so it's important to gauge our learners' perceptions here. We also will want to be sure that we are using job aids in the most beneficial way. Having a question on our smile sheet forces us to avoid sliding into the comfort of denial. Furthermore, if we include this question, we send a stealth message to all our stakeholders about the importance of job aids and other prompting mechanisms. For every training session or every elearning program, our trainers and instructional designers will get feedback about job-aid use. In every training-effectiveness review by learning leaders, job-aid utilization will be examined. In every report to senior managers, they too will be reminded that job aids are a critical element of learning solutions. To reiterate, by including such questions on our smile sheets—even if we could answer the question ourselves with no assist from our learners—we unleash powerful ripples of guidance that remind all of us of our critical performance-focused responsibilities. Uplifting music fades . . .

### *After-Learning Follow-Through—Tertiary Goal—Supervisor Follow-up*

Supervisors are organizational superglue. They have the power to keep organizational actors focused, to engender passionate effort and creativity, to troubleshoot problems, and to help coordinate disparate limbs of the organizational octopus.

They can also screw things up big time! We've all heard about this. "People don't quit their company; they quit their managers." "My supervisor wasn't born on planet Earth; he was born on Space Station Dilbert." Et cetera! Even these negative stories tell of the power of supervisors.

Supervisors are also powerful agents in training and development. As Salas, Tannenbaum, Kraiger, and Smith-Jentsch said in their seminal research review:

> *[Researchers have] found that one misdirected comment by a team leader can wipe out the full effects of a training program. . . . What organizations ought to do is provide [supervisors] with information they need to (a) guide trainees to the right*

*training, (b) clarify trainees' expectations, (c) prepare trainees, and (d) reinforce learning. . . . (p. 83)*

*Salas et al. further note that supervisors can increase trainees' motivation to engage in the learning process (p. 85).*

*After trainees have completed training, supervisors should be positive about training, remove obstacles, and ensure ample opportunity for trainees to apply what they have learned and receive feedback. . . . (p. 90)*

*Transfer is directly related to opportunities to practice— opportunities provided either by the direct supervisor or the organization. (p. 90)*

---

**Question 123**

**In what ways to do you expect your supervisor will support you in applying what you learned to your job?**

**Circle as many items as are true.**

    A.  My supervisor will allow me to implement what I learned.

    B.  My supervisor will give me additional time, if it is needed, to enable me to implement what I learned.

    C.  My supervisor will give me additional resources, if they are needed, to enable me to implement what I learned.

    D.  My supervisor will actively encourage me to implement what I learned.

    E.  My supervisor will coach me, or find a coach for me, to help me implement what I learned.

    F.  My supervisor will assign me with a work project where I will be expected to utilize my new knowledge and skills.

    G.  My supervisor will work with me to set goals for implementing what I learned.

    H.  My supervisor will monitor my progress in implementing what I learned.

    I.  My supervisor will ensure that I am provided with additional learning opportunities to deepen my understanding.

    J.  Unfortunately, my supervisor is not likely to provide much support to help me implement what I learned.

    K.  Unfortunately, my supervisor is likely to make it more difficult for me to implement what I learned.

---

Holy chocolate cannoli, Batman! Is that a freakin' great list of supervisor imperatives or what? This book may be more than just a book on smile sheets.

Seriously, though, that list is a great tool to educate supervisors about how they can maximize learning ~~transfer~~ application.[27] You, of course, could utilize such a list in a leadership-development course—but perhaps you don't have to, if you use this list in a smile-sheet question and then feed the results back to your supervisors. Such stealth messaging will make the case for you and will make it over and over and over again—not one time as a typical leadership-development course might do. Of course, no harm in doing both!

Standards for this question might have choices A and J as unacceptable and choice K as completely unacceptable. Choices B, C, and D are acceptable. Choices E, F, G, H, and I are superior.

## Chapter Summary

Wow! So many great smile-sheet questions! They make me wonder—perhaps they make you wonder, too—why have we relied on such pathetic smile-sheet questions in the past? Honestly, I can't tell you. Perhaps tradition? Perhaps the easy face-validity of the old questions? I don't know, but for whatever reason traditional smile-sheet questions were not designed with a performance focus. They were not designed with questions that enabled actionable results.

The questions presented in this chapter may not always reach our ideals of perfection, but they're infinitely better than traditional smile-sheet questions. They're better because:

1. They are based on the learning research.

2. They help learners make better smile-sheet decisions.

3. They are actionable.

4. They communicate more clearly to stakeholders.

5. They help us educate stakeholders through stealth messaging.

---

27  "Transfer" is for training weenies like us—not for supervisors or other organizational stakeholders.

The wisdom that underlies the structure of the four pillars was derived over more than a decade through in-depth research reviews and practical application. To make learning research usable and practical it has to be simplified to its core elements. The four pillars—understanding, remembering, motivation to apply, and after-training follow-through—can't possibly encompass every factor relevant to the workplace learning landscape, but they encompass a huge percentage of what is practically important. By basing the questions on the four-pillar model, we will ensure that our smile sheets are focused on on-the-job performance and will produce actionable results.

# CHAPTER 7

## DELAYED SMILE SHEETS

A T SEVERAL POINTS EARLIER IN THIS BOOK, I mentioned delayed smile sheets. Here in this chapter I'm going to focus on them in more detail—because they deserve to be observed from an elevated vista above the haze of other considerations.

Delayed smile sheets tell us things that end-of-training smile sheets cannot. They give learners an entirely different perspective from which to make their smile-sheet decisions. In particular, delayed smile sheets:

1. Help learners overcome the top-of-mind problem that occurs with end-of-training smile sheets. Specifically, they enable learners to evaluate **how well they've remembered** what they learned.

2. Help learners see on-the-job **practical outcomes** that they cannot see within training.

3. Help learners rethink **the value** of the training in light of how well their learning-implementation efforts have gone.

4. Enable learners to report on their **actual successes and failures** in attempting to implement the learning.

5. Enable learners to report on the **specific obstacles** they've faced and the **success factors** that enabled them to reach their learning-implementation goals.

These insights are huge! Especially given that our whole goal with Performance-Focused Smile Sheets is to produce on-the-job performance improvement. Delayed smile sheets give us more of a window into the job situation than an end-of-training smile sheet could ever give us.

## Benefits of Delayed Smile Sheets

The five-item list above outlines the different perspectives that learners gain from delayed smile sheets. These perspectives lead to a variety of benefits, which we'll now discuss.

When learning is measured at the end of training, memory retrieval is artificially enhanced. When learners' perspectives on their own learning are measured at the end of training—as they are on end-of-training smile sheets—learners suffer from a top-of-mind bias that makes them think that the learning is more effective than it actually is. The best way to reduce these biases is to also provide learners with delayed measures of learning—and delayed smile sheets. Delayed smile sheets ensure that learning is not top of mind for the learners, but is more representative of their on-the-job cognitions. Because of this, learners will have greater insight about the potency of the training to support their remembering and their ability to apply what they have learned on the job.

When learners are back on their jobs and are asked to evaluate a previous training program, they know whether they've attempted to apply the new concepts or not. They know whether they've encountered situations that are relevant to the training topics covered previously. If they did make extra efforts to apply what they've learned, they know how successful they've been. These perspectives enable the learners to reflect with clear eyes on the relevance and value of the training.

Delayed smile sheets also give learners an opportunity to report on their successes and failures. Both can help other learners be more successful in implementing their own learning. Success stories can be gathered to motivate and guide others in their own efforts. Failures can be explored for lessons learned, enabling others to navigate difficulties. If desired, capturing successes and failures and their organizational implications—for example, using Brinkerhoff's Success Case Method or Phillips's ROI data-gathering protocols—can provide feedback to the organization on the cost-benefit implications of training-inspired actions.

Finally, and very powerfully, delayed smile sheets can capture information about the obstacles and success factors learners have faced in applying what they've learned. This is particularly useful because the information gathered about obstacles and success factors can (a) help instructional designers address weaknesses in the training and maintain its strengths, (b) help work-learning professionals improve training deployment and after-training support strategies, and (c) inform business-line managers and learners' supervisors about improvements they can make to support learning implementation.

## Special Logistics for Delayed Smile Sheets

I recommend delivering delayed smile sheets between two and four weeks after training ends. These time boundaries are not definitive—they could be a little bit shorter or a little bit longer—but they are designed to balance the need to give learners time to apply what they've learned and the need to ensure that training wasn't delivered so long ago that the learning process has become completely irrelevant to the learners.

In this day of easy online survey software, delayed smile sheets will almost always be delivered electronically. While some organizations require that these instruments be delivered behind a firewall, I'm not sure I fully understand the need for such high security. The questions you use are likely to be similar to the questions that other companies will use—and the data you gather on your smile sheets are highly unlikely to contain any critical intellectual property. There's no reason not to use survey software like SurveyMonkey—at least in terms of security. On the other hand, you may want to connect your findings to your Learning Management System, especially if it's running Experience API (a software module, sometimes called "Tin Can," that enables extensive data-collection possibilities).

Delayed smile sheets can often use some of the same questions that a standard Performance-Focused Smile Sheet uses—although sometimes slight changes of wording will be required to make the questions make sense.

For example, on our regular smile sheet we would ask:

- In what ways do you expect your supervisor will support you in applying what you learned to your job?

On our delayed smile sheet we would modify it to say:

- In what ways did your supervisor support you in applying what you learned to your job?

Indeed, this consanguinity can be useful in comparing learner's expectations to actual outcomes. For example, look at the two question options above. It might be very interesting to compare what learners expect from their supervisors and what supervisors actually deliver. The implications of sharing this kind of data with organizational actors are massive. And, I'm not just talking about this example. I'm talking about all the comparisons we might conjure between the results of end-of-training smile sheets and the delayed smile sheets.

One pushback I sometimes get when I advocate for delayed smile sheets is that learners don't have time to complete another survey. This is a fundamental issue, one not to be dismissed lightly. We're talking about two critical things here: the potential for actual productivity loss and the reputation of us learning professionals as time vacuums. There are several considerations worth reflecting on.

First, how much actual time does it take folks to complete a delayed smile sheet? If we figure an average of sixty seconds per question, we're talking about ten to fifteen minutes, depending on the length of the delayed smile sheet. The question then becomes, what value is there in that time investment? For traditional smile sheets there was zero value in the results—because nothing ever changed and no valuable information was uncovered. But with better questions, we will be able to provide real value. It might, however, take us some time and change-management effort to demonstrate that value. We'll talk more about how we should do that in the next chapter.

Second, we may have to compromise and deliver delayed smile sheets only for high-importance training programs or only for a few pilot programs at first until we can prove their value. We may have to prioritize our questions and cut out questions so as to use less time. Finally, perhaps we need to think in terms of a cultural change in the way we deliver training and the value we create. Certainly we need to educate our stakeholders in the value of these types of performance-focused interventions. But perhaps delayed smile sheets could become part of a larger strategic learning renaissance within your organization. At a minimum, we will have to convince our learners—the folks who will decide whether to give their time to our delayed smile sheets—that their additional investment is worth it.

One final thought for this section on the logistics of delayed smile sheets. Many organizations do this funny thing in trying to follow the Kirkpatrick Model. Specifically, in wanting to go beyond Level 1, learner reactions, and Level 2, tests of learning—to get to Level 3, on-the-job behavior—they essentially send out delayed smile sheets and declare the results as Level 3 results. They ask learners about whether they've been able to apply the learning successfully and they inappropriately transmogrify these responses into an index of actual on-the-job performance. If you've gotten this far in the book—and if you have read about the problems with self-report data—you'll readily see how this *behaviorization*[28] of smile-sheet data is an entirely dubious enterprise. Let me put this simply: Delayed smile sheets are not good measures of on-the-job behavior. They don't align with Kirkpatrick's Level 3. To measure on-the-job behavior accurately, we must do more than ask learners to evaluate their own learning application.

## Additional Question Opportunities

In addition to standard Performance-Focused Smile-Sheet questions, delayed smile sheets should offer an additional set of questions, starting with the *pivot question*:[29,30]

---

28  I'm using the made up word "behaviorization" to represent the practice of turning data from learners' opinions into behavioral data at Level 3 of the Kirkpatrick taxonomy.

29  Another variant of this question is a five-item question with two affirmative responses as follows: D. Yes, I HAVE ALREADY USED what I learned (ONCE OR TWICE). E. Yes, I HAVE REPEATEDLY USED what I learned.

30  I call this a "pivot question" because it enables us to pivot toward two or more follow-up questions, based on the answer given by the respondent.

**Question 124**

**Have you used what you learned in the training to make a significant improvement in your work?**

    A.  NO, and I DOUBT THAT I WILL USE what I learned.

    B.  NO, BUT I PROBABLY WILL USE what I learned.

    C.  NO, BUT I HAVE A SPECIFIC PLAN TO USE what I learned.

    D.  YES, I HAVE ALREADY USED what I learned.

Pivot questions like this one let our delayed smile sheet branch to one of two follow-up questions. If learners answer "no"—if they select one of the first three answer choices above—we give them a question that asks them what is holding them back from being successful. If they answer "yes," we give them a question that asks them what success factors enabled them to be successful. The logic of the branching is shown in the diagram that follows

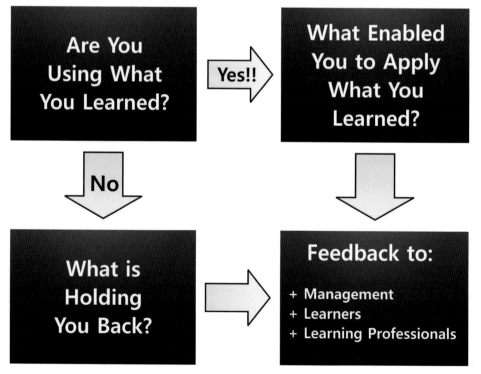

**Delayed smile sheets can provide critical feedback for management, learners, and learning professionals like us.**

Let's examine the two post-pivot questions. First, we'll look at a follow-up question when learners say they have been successful.

---

**Question 125**

**Select the top 3 or 4 factors that have enabled you to put the training's learning points into practice to make beneficial on-the-job improvements?**

    A.  My management has made this a high priority.

    B.  I have decided to lead a change effort to make this happen.

    C.  I believe strongly in the workshop's learning points.

    D.  I will be sanctioned or punished if I do NOT do this.

    E.  My management is fully supportive of my efforts.

    F.  I have the authority to make necessary changes.

    G.  My coworkers are fully supportive of my efforts.

    H.  I will be acknowledged or rewarded if I do this.

    I.  I remember (or can look up) the workshop's learning points.

    J.  My team (or our whole unit) is working together on this.

    K.  I have the time to put this into practice.

    L.  I have the resources to put this into practice.

    M.  Other (please specify)_____

---

The answer choices—because they do not have an inherent order—can be randomized (except for the last choice, the "Other" choice). And note that the "Other" choice is very important because you might find for your organization that there are special success factors that are critical. If you capture what people write in for the "Other" response, you'll be able to hardwire it in on a later version of the survey. And please, let me know if you found another critical success factor—so I can let the world know. Thanks!

The following question can be used when learners state they have not yet put their learning into practice.

---

**Question 126**

**What is holding you back from using what you have learned to make changes in your work?**

    A.  The learning content is not relevant to my current job.

    B.  I don't think the learning content is valid.

    C.  I don't see how making the changes will benefit me.

    D.  I don't know how to make the case for change.

    E.  I don't have the authority to make changes.

    F.  I'm not comfortable leading such a change effort.

    G.  I can't remember the learning content well enough.

    H.  I'm not sure I know enough to take the next steps.

    I.  I haven't had the time.

    J.  I have had higher priorities.

    K.  I have not had the resources.

    L.  The risk of making these changes is too high.

    M.  I'm still working to persuade management.

    N.  I'm still working to persuade my teammates.

    O.  I have been blocked by management.

    P.  Others around me don't support the changes.

    Q.  Other (please specify)_____

---

Hmm. Funny that I found more obstacles than success factors, isn't it? Note that the same options apply in this question as in the previous one—you can randomize the answer choices, and the "Other" choice is critical to gather additional obstacles that folks may be encountering in your organization.

Also, if you want to use this question for people who have stated they have begun to apply their training—just to make sure you capture all the obstacles—you can change the wording of the question to, "What obstacles, if any, have made it challenging to apply your learning?"

### Feedback to Key Stakeholders

The pivot question and the two post-pivot questions can provide critical—and sometimes urgent—feedback to key stakeholder groups. I've experienced this in conducting my own workshops. For example, I found in one company that the learners who had already begun implementing the learning were motivated by a management-driven initiative. I learned this based on the learners' responses to the questions. I was then able to feed that insight back to the training manager at the company and tell her that she needed to continue to actively lead the initiative—because otherwise her folks might not continue in applying what they had learned.

This feedback can be valuable not just to learning executives, instructional designers, and trainers but also to line leaders, learners' supervisors, and the learners themselves. Imagine the power in sending messages like these:

To learners:

- "Sixty-eight percent of you have already successfully applied what you learned."
- "The two most important success factors that have propelled those who have been successful are _____."
- "The biggest obstacle your cohort has faced is _____. What advice do you have for your colleagues who are hung up on this obstacle?"

To learners' managers:

- From the CEO: "Along with Chief Learning Officer Holting, I've reviewed the recent feedback on the Excelsior Training Class. While this may not reflect on you as an individual supervisor, many direct reports from the Excelsior Training indicate that supervisors are one of the biggest obstacles they are facing in applying what they've learned. Specifically, they don't feel they have the authority to make changes. Here's my recommendation: Work with your direct reports to set training-implementation goals, grant them the authority to implement what they've learned, see what help they need, and follow up with them in two weeks to ensure they're making progress. As you know, Excelsior is one of the keys to our continued strategic success. I'm counting on you as supervisors to make this program successful."

- From the course instructors: "Good news! Your direct reports— the ones who took my February class—tell me that most of you are doing a great job supporting them in applying their new learning on the job. Keep up the good work, and if you feel you're having difficulty, please let me know, as I want to ensure that everyone is successful."

To instructional designers and/or trainers:

- "Houston, we have a problem. More than 50% of the learners don't value the content in Course 392. We're going to have to take a deeper look."

- "On Course 582, about 40% of the class seems stuck because they don't have enough time to apply what they've learned. Let's get together with the head of Marketing and see if there's anything we can do on our end. Perhaps we could provide a booster session after they get through their big crunch. Or maybe Marketing management will want to make changes at their end to enable the learners who need it to have a little more learning-application time."

Asking learners about whether they've been successful in applying what they've learned is the most critical pivot question, but it's not the only pivot question that is useful. For example, I've used a second pivot question some-times—"Have you taught others what you've learned?"—and found the results illuminating. Certainly, one goal for some training classes is that the learners share what they've learned with others. By using the "have-you-taught" pivot question, we can both assess how successful we've been in encouraging such sharing and also send stealth messages that sharing is part of what's expected.

In addition to the two pivot questions I've mentioned, there may be other critical questions that you might ask. Be sure to let me know if you come up with another valuable pivot question.

## Summary: The Benefits of Delayed Smile Sheets

Delayed smile sheets make sense, they're not hard to implement, and they provide real and undeniable value. We may have to spend a little political capital to get them implemented at first, but the rewards to our organizations will likely be large and self-reinforcing.

By using delayed smile sheets, we send several key messages to our organization, including the following:

1. Training isn't successful until learning is applied to the job.

2. Learners often need support and encouragement to apply what they've learned.

3. Learners must take responsibility for after-training efforts.

4. Learners' managers can provide critical after-training support.

5. Learners may face obstacles in implementing what they've learned—obstacles that should be targeted to be overcome.

6. Success factors for implementing new concepts should be catalogued and parlayed into additional successes.

Delayed smile sheets provide a more realistic view of the worth of training—a view tempered by real-world after-training experience. They overcome the biases inherent in top-of-mind responding during training. They give workplace professionals, learners, and learners' managers feedback on how learning application is going—enabling midcourse corrections that can significantly improve the outcomes of learning.

# CHAPTER 8

## HOW TO PRESENT YOUR SMILE-SHEET RESULTS

UP TILL THIS POINT, WE HAVE FOCUSED on gathering data. But, of course, we also have to present data—to both our stakeholders and ourselves. This chapter illustrates how to do this effectively.

Where traditional smile-sheet data are often transformed into meaningless numbers, Performance-Focused Smile Sheets can present results that inform, elucidate, and engender urgency and action. It's really not difficult. Mostly, we just have to present the results as they are. This, of course, provides an advantage—because with minimal transformation, there is less loss of meaning than with traditional smile sheets.

Here's the job-aid question we looked at earlier.

---

**Using job aids, checklists, or other prompting mechanisms can be an effective way to ensure you properly apply skills to your job. Which of the following are true?**

**Circle as many items as are true.**

A. We did NOT RECEIVE ANY WORTHWHILE job aids, checklists, or similar prompting mechanisms to direct our on-the-job actions.

B. We RECEIVED ONE OR MORE WORTHWHILE job aids, checklists, or similar prompting mechanisms.

C. During the course, we USED ONE OR MORE WORTHWHILE job aids, checklists, or similar prompting mechanisms in REALISTIC PRACTICE EXERCISES.

D. Between sessions of our course, IN OUR WORKSITES, WE UTILIZED one or more WORTHWHILE job aids, checklists, or similar prompting mechanisms IN A REAL-WORLD JOB TASK.

---

And here's a graph displaying results for this question:

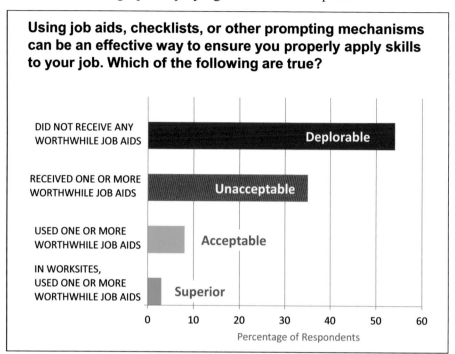

The power in such a graphic is self-evident. Note the answer choices first. They clearly distinguish between different realities. Learners either received a worthwhile job aid or they did not. They either used a job aid during learning or they did not. There are no squishy comparisons between "agree" and "strongly agree" to numb us into inaction. Also note the red warning signs and the green signal of success. How could someone miss these color signals? And note the adjectives on each data point, letting us know when a result is acceptable or not.

There are several things to note about how to make such a graph. First, I was able to easily use the chart function in PowerPoint to create this exhibit. I had to adjust the chart outputs a bit to improve the chart's appearance, but it didn't take long. Moreover, once you get the settings right, you can just make duplicates by copying your original chart and then changing the data.

Second, the answer choices as displayed on the chart were shortened to enable quick readability. Care has to be taken in doing this so that you don't lose or distort the meaning or significance of the answer choices. Indeed, it may be useful to offer your audience the full question on a separate slide or document if you decide to shorten the answer choices.

Third, the data bars have been color coded and labeled with the question standards to ensure that viewers get a clear message about the level of acceptability of the answer choices. Note too that you'll have to plan in advance the words you use for your standards. Here, I'm using "Deplorable," "Unacceptable," "Acceptable," and "Superior;" but you may prefer a different set of labels for your standards. The key is to figure out *first*—before you even develop your smile sheet—what labels you'll use for your standards. If you create labels after you have the data, you're opening up the process to bias and political pressure.

You'll note that the chart does not use a legend. Legends are a poor design choice because they force viewers to look back and forth between the data and the label, overwhelming working memory. Where possible, put the label on or near the actual data.

Finally, note that for select-as-many-as-you-like questions, labels like the "Unacceptable" choice in the graph—"Received one or more worthwhile job aids"—will need an explanation. In this instance, it's not unacceptable if learners get a worthwhile job aid; it's unacceptable if that's all they get. Learners should also be asked to use the job aid in the training program itself.

## Comparing Current Findings to Previous Findings

While these questions can stand alone, you may also want to compare the current results to previous results to uncover trends. You can do that within the same kind of chart, as shown here.

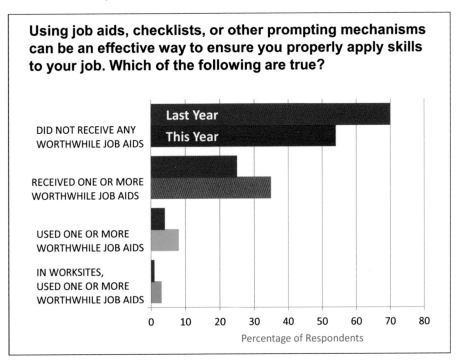

Note that it's probably not good to show this comparison chart first. By showing the noncomparison visual first, and then showing this comparison view, you will help your viewers focus initially on the current findings and then compare those findings to the previous year's findings. This tactic is helpful because it gets your viewers to look deeply at the current situation rather than focusing on the year-to-year differences.

### Providing Summary Data Using a Single Question

Looking at the findings for individual questions is great to get folks to focus on critical issues, but you may want to provide some overall summation of the findings as well. There are two ways to do this. First, you can designate one question (or maybe two or three) as the one that best provides an overall sense of the success of your training program. You won't be surprised by my choice. I recommend the World's Best Smile Sheet Question as the most indicative of the overall success of a training program.

Here it is again.

---

**In regard to the course topics taught, HOW ABLE ARE YOU to put what you've learned into practice on the job?**

    A. I'm NOT AT ALL ABLE to put the concepts into practice.

    B. I have GENERAL AWARENESS of the concepts taught, but I WILL NEED MORE TRAINING / PRACTICE / GUIDANCE / EXPERIENCE TO DO ACTUAL JOB TASKS using the concepts taught.

    C. I am ABLE TO WORK ON ACTUAL JOB TASKS, but I'LL NEED MORE HANDS-ON EXPERIENCE to be fully competent in using the concepts taught.

    D. I am ABLE TO PERFORM ACTUAL JOB TASKS at a FULLY COMPETENT LEVEL in using the concepts taught.

    E. I am ABLE TO PERFORM ACTUAL JOB TASKS at an EXPERT LEVEL in using the concepts taught.

---

The following graph depicts how this might look presented with its results.

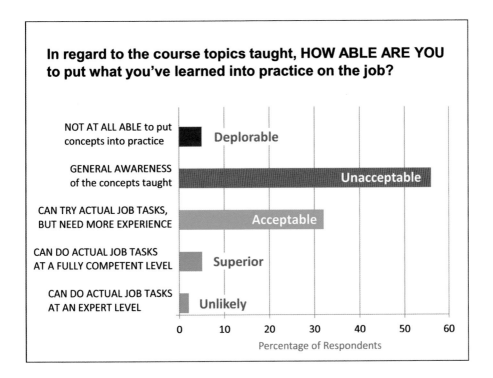

## Providing Summary Data Using Acceptability Indexing

Instead of using one question, you could create an index using multiple questions—all indexed to the four pillars discussed earlier: (1) understanding, (2) remembering, (3) motivation to apply, and (4) after-training follow-through. To create an index for these, you would first decide which question—or which questions—would be used to calculate a score for each of the four pillars.

Then, for each question, you would calculate the percentage of responses that met the minimum standard for acceptability. Finally, if you were using more than one question to calculate a score for one of the four pillars, you would average the percentage of acceptable-or-better responses.

Let's look at an example.

We'll begin with the first pillar, Understanding. Suppose we were going to use the following question as our sole index of Understanding.

> **Now that you've taken the course, how well do you understand the concepts taught in the course?**
>
> A. I have some significant CONFUSIONS AND/OR BLIND SPOTS.
>
> B. I have a BASIC FAMILIARITY with the concepts.
>
> C. I have a SOLID UNDERSTANDING of the concepts.
>
> D. I have a COMPREHENSIVE UNDERSTANDING of the concepts.
>
> E. I have an EXPERT-LEVEL UNDERSTANDING of the concepts.

Suppose further that only choices C, D, and E were deemed acceptable (or better than acceptable) and we got the following percentages:

| | | |
|---|---|---|
| A. | CONFUSIONS AND/OR BLIND SPOTS: | 5% |
| B. | BASIC FAMILIARITY: | 60% |
| C. | SOLID UNDERSTANDING: | 25% |
| D. | COMPREHENSIVE UNDERSTANDING: | 10% |
| E. | EXPERT-LEVEL UNDERSTANDING: | 0% |

**CALCULATED ACCEPTABILITY INDEX—**
**for UNDERSTANDING:**                                    **35%**

By adding up the percentages for the acceptable responses—choices C, D, E—we would have an acceptability index for Understanding at 35%.

For the second pillar, Remembering, let's suppose we wanted to use the three tertiary questions recommended earlier. We would calculate the acceptability index for each question and then take an average. For example:

1. Realistic Retrieval Practice    Acceptability Index:    36%

2. Spaced Repetitions    Acceptability Index:    25%

3. Situation-Action Triggering    Acceptability Index:    5%

**CALCULATED ACCEPTABILITY INDEX—**
**for REMEMBERING:**                                    **22%**

You could, of course, get fancier and utilize weighted averaging, but simple is often better because simple is easier to explain.

Suppose you continued further and calculated acceptability indices for all four pillars and for the World's Best Smile Sheet Question. You could then display your results, for example, on a PowerPoint slide, as shown here.

| Targets | Acceptability Indices GOALS for THIS YEAR | Acceptability Indices ACHIEVED THIS YEAR |
|---|---|---|
| Overall Question | 50% | 39% |
| Understanding | 60% | 35% |
| Remembering | 35% | 22% |
| Motivation to Apply | 70% | 57% |
| After-Learning Follow-Through | 45% | 24% |

Note the idea in the chart that goals can be created for these acceptability indices and current performance can be judged against those goals. As we all know, goals facilitate motivation, effectiveness, and goal-relevant performance.

Note that while I did not color-code the chart above, you could do that as well, providing shades of green and red depending on how well the results meet the acceptability thresholds. One piece of advice: If you don't have a talent for creating aesthetically appealing visuals, you might want to find a graphic designer to help you plan the colors.

## Complications in Calculating Acceptability Indices

The questions for which we've calculated acceptability indices have required relatively straightforward calculations. Unfortunately, not all questions will be so easy. Take the case of the question we looked at earlier related to "applying learning to the job."

---

**After the course, when you begin to apply your new knowledge at your worksite, which of the following supports are likely to be in place for you?**

**Circle as many items as are likely to be true.**

A.  I will have ENOUGH TIME to work on applying what I learned.

B.  I will be ENCOURAGED BY MY SUPERVISOR to apply what I learned to real job tasks.

C.  I will have my PROGRESS MONITORED BY MY SUPERVISOR in applying what I learned.

D.  I will have someone available TO COACH OR MENTOR ME on applying what I learned.

E.  I will have easy access to FELLOW LEARNERS to contact for guidance and support.

F.  I will have easy access to a COURSE INSTRUCTOR to contact for guidance and support.

G.  I will be ENCOURAGED BY MY COWORKERS to apply what I learned to real job tasks.

H.  I will have JOB AIDS to guide me in applying what I learned to real job tasks.

I.  I will be PERIODICALLY REMINDED of key learning concepts/ skills through some systematic after-learning intervention(s).

J.  I will NOT get much direct support, but will rely on my own initiative.

---

To calculate an acceptability rating for such a question, you will first have to determine which answer choices qualify as acceptable. When we discussed this question earlier, I had anointed choices A through I as acceptable—with only choice J being unacceptable. The tricky part is that if a learner chooses only one or two of the acceptable answer choices, we might not deem that as acceptable; we might want learners to have the benefit of at least three of these after-training supports, for example. Unfortunately, if we want the learners to select more than one choice for their response to merit overall acceptability, then we will experience some mathematical complications. In particular, we won't be able to simply add up the percentage responses received by each answer choice. To make the calculation, we would have to look at each learner's set of responses and decide whether they merit an overall acceptability rating. To calculate this manually, you may have to download the data into a spreadsheet or other software program or eyeball each respondent's answers separately for this type of question. Alternatively, you could rewrite the question or use another question to avoid this calculation difficulty. Not to worry, though! Remember, we're not seeking perfection, but validity with workability.

## Summary: Sharing Smile-Sheet Results

In this chapter, I attempted to give you some ideas and guidelines about how to report the smile-sheet data. As I hope I made clear, this is not a throwaway task but an extremely critical one.

I have identified nine keys to reporting the data:

1. Share all the data gathered or you'll introduce bias into the process. The corollary to this is that you should not gather data that you're not going to share.

2. Before presenting the data, share the four-pillar model to ensure your audience knows why you're tracking what you're tracking.

3. Also, share the standards for acceptability to guide and support your audience's interpretation of the data.

4. When sharing the results, first examine each of the smile-sheet questions separately—because each has been designed to get at a specific critical aspect of training design, deployment, and follow-through. Wait to share any summary data.

5. Use good visual design principles in sharing the data, especially putting labels near the data, keeping the visual as uncluttered as possible, and seeking to send clear messages through the visual design elements.

6. Integrate the concept of acceptability into your visuals, letting your audience know where the data show good results and where the data show poor results. In other words, don't just share the data without framing its meaning.

7. Consider using (a) the World's Best Smile Sheet Question and (b) acceptability indices for the four pillars in a summary report.

8. Consider setting goals for your acceptability indices and comparing current results to those goals.

9. Consider comparing current results to previous results to see if outcomes are trending in the right direction.

# Chapter 9

# Making This Happen

THE IDEAS IN THIS BOOK ARE FREAKIN' revolutionary. That's both good news and bad news. It's good news because the old way of doing smile sheets just wasn't working. It's bad news because now that you've read this book, you too are out on the bleeding edge of the revolution—unless you're reading this somewhere ages and ages hence, and then this warning won't make all that much difference.

Revolutions are difficult. Mere change efforts are difficult. This is no time for an extended dissertation on how to lead a change effort. Instead, I'm going to keep this short and sweet and target this for those of you who want to bring Performance-Focused Smile Sheets to your organization.

## Arguments to Make Your Case

Providing rational arguments is worth a try—even if they don't always work that well. This book, in some sense, is a rational argument, so if you want to craft your own argument, you might want to borrow heavily from the arguments in this book. Here are some shortcuts:

1. **You:** "Our current smile sheets have the following flaws: (1) they are not designed based on research-based best practices and are not aligned with how workplace learning actually works to support on-the-job performance; (2) they use poorly constructed questions, often with fuzzy answer choices; and (3) they don't support our learners in actually answering the questions—so our

smile sheets suffer from the garbage-in, garbage-out problem. Indeed, scientists who have studied smile sheets like ours have found them almost completely uncorrelated with learning! Fortunately, this gorgeous man-hunk of a learning consultant, Dr. Will Thalheimer—who's also a brilliant, humble humanitarian—has developed a new research-based design for smile sheets: the Performance-Focused Smile Sheet."

2.  **You:** "What is our primary goal in workplace learning? If we had to choose between creating highly rated training or creating actual on-the-job performance improvement, wouldn't we choose performance improvement? But what do our current smile sheets focus on? They focus on training; they focus on the classroom; they focus on elearning. It's time we updated our smile sheets to be more performance focused. Fortunately . . ."

3.  **Them:** "But smile sheets really aren't that important. Why are we spending any time on them?"
    **You:** "As business leaders have so wisely observed, 'what gets measured, gets managed.' Now it's true that most smile sheets aren't used to actually manage anything, but that's a function of the quality of the data they've been producing. There's a new method for creating smile sheets that will actually help us gather meaningful data—data that we can use to make our training more effective and more efficient."

4.  **Them:** "But won't better smile sheets take more time and resources?"
    **You:** "No, not really. They'll actually help save time and money by giving us the feedback we need to make our training programs significantly better, wildly better, orders of magnitude better! How many trainings have you been to where you forgot most of what you learned after a couple of weeks? Or, how many trainings do we have in this organization that get people all pumped up but then send them back to work where they're overwhelmed, where they get no support to implement what they

learned in training, where the momentum from the training basically fades away? Well, these new smile sheets will actually track critical factors in training that support long-term performance. "Specifically, these Performance-Focused Smile Sheets—that's what they're called—index data under four key factors that link training to performance outcomes: (1) Do the learners actually understand what they're learning well enough to make job-relevant decisions and successfully apply job-relevant skills? (2) Do the learners actually remember what they've learned, because if they don't remember it, we've wasted a ton of money? (3) Are the learners invested in what they've learned; are they motivated to take what they've learned and use it in their jobs? (4) Are there after-training supports in place to remind learners of what they learned, guide them to appropriate actions even when they can't remember everything, keep them motivated to follow through, and provide them with guidance, support, and oversight to propel their success? These four key success factors—understanding, remembering, motivation-to-apply, and after-training follow-through—are used to design the questions used on the smile sheet. So now, if we use the new smile sheet design, we'll actually get smile-sheet data that means something. Finally, these Performance-Focused Smile Sheets were inspired by the scientific research on learning—which is more than we can say for our current smile sheets."

5. **Them:** "But won't these Performance-Focused Smile Sheets make some of our trainers and instructional designers uncomfortable?"
   **You:** "Yes, they will. Damn right! Two things about that. First, they'll make our weakest trainers and instructional designers nervous because they'll finally be held accountable for performance. Because our current smile sheets are uncorrelated with learning results, nobody can be held accountable. Not even me. For our best and brightest, however, these new smile sheets will be a breath of fresh air. For years, our best folks have been pushing for better learning designs, but the organization hasn't been responsive because the data leaves all of us in the dark about costs and benefits. We've

even lost some of our best people when they've seen we weren't going to implement proven learning designs. With the new smile sheets—and the better feedback loops that they enable—our best and brightest will be able to innovate to actually drive improved on-the-job performance. Not only that, but the insights from the new data will help our best and brightest learn more quickly in their work, creating a more responsive improvement cycle. Our best and brightest will love the cultural change engendered by the new smile sheets! And, we'll gradually get a reputation as a great place to do good work, with all of the recruiting benefits that implies. "Second, change is hard. This change may be resisted at first. We'll all be a touch uncomfortable, but we'll get through it—to a much better place."

6.  **Them:** "What's the business case for using these new smile sheets?" **You**: "The bottom line is that the new smile sheets are going to make our training much, much more effective. That, in turn, will help our folks perform better, be more innovative, waste less time doing the wrong things, waste less time in training that has little impact, and enable our organization to succeed. That's the standard business case argument, but here's another way to look at this. Performance-Focused Smile Sheets create a competitive advantage. If our competition starts using these before we do, they'll accelerate their learning-based job improvement before we do—and this is likely to be subject to reciprocal causality—a snowball effect. Improvements will get magnified with every iteration. If our competition gets started first in improving their learning results, we may not be able to catch up for years!"

### Suggestions for Getting Started

Your great persuasion skills notwithstanding, arguments will only get you so far. One of the best ways to get traction in any change initiative is to try stuff out, experiment a little, pilot something to learn how it works and how to make it work better. Fly under the radar until you have some data to show that the new way of doing things is having an impact in your organization.

Find one or two trainers and/or instructional designers who want to try this out—people who are really hungry to learn and are open to honest (and maybe even harsh) feedback as long as it's informative. Roll it out for their courses. Praise their initiative. Let them talk to you and to their colleagues about what they learned. Make improvements based on their insights. Gather their testimonials.

Another way to think about this is to frame the Performance-Focused Smile Sheet as part of a larger strategic initiative to look for ways to improve your training-and-development results. You know what you need to do here! First, gather information. Use the Performance-Focused Smile Sheet as one of several data-gathering techniques to capture baseline data and look for blind spots. Second, begin to reeducate your workplace learning-and-performance team to be more focused on performance improvement. With your full team, build a new strategic vision. As you begin implementing the new strategic vision for workplace learning, continue to use the Performance-Focused Smile Sheet to gauge your progress.

## Caveats and Warnings

Traditional smile sheets are a clear and present danger to our field. A much better option—as this book demonstrates—are Performance-Focused Smile Sheets. But, my dear reader, let me remind you of a key idea that I have already emphasized with rough language and insightful argumentation. Smile sheets *are not* and *cannot* provide us with all the feedback we need as workplace professionals. Neither can they provide full information to our organizations, to our clients, or to our learners. Nor can we rely on the Kirkpatrick four-level model or the Phillips five-level ROI model or Kauffman's six-level societal-impact model, or any of their variants. In a later book, I hope to share my work on Full-Source Learning Evaluation, but for now let me just list some of the key aspects we can also measure as learning professionals:

- On-the-job behavior targeted for performance improvement

- On-the-job behavior not specifically targeted for performance improvement

- Factors that support and enable on-the-job behavior

- Factors that hinder on-the-job behavior

- Learner understanding

- Learner remembering

- Realistic decision-making performance

- Validity, deployment, use, and effectiveness of prompting mechanisms

- On-the-job learning support for remembering

- On-the-job learning support for just-in-time learning

- On-the-job learning support for prompting

- Learner benefits

- Organizational results

So, I beg of you, please do *not* end your learning-measurement efforts with smile sheets. Have I been clear enough about this?

### My Best Wishes

Thank you! Thank you for reading this far, for listening to my ideas, and for occasionally laughing at my jokes (I hope!). My goal in writing this book is to get us to improve our learning-and-performance results—and to get us to reinvent our smile sheets, taking them more seriously as the change lever that they can be.

I hope you'll put some or all of this into practice. Please feel free to let me know how I can help—and just as importantly, let me know how it's going! I would love to hear your success stories, your lessons learned, and your improvements. I've spent years thinking about this, but what I've learned along the way is that I'm always able to make things better. Please help me in that.

Good luck and may you gather good folks to work with you on this. Pushing for change is much more pleasant and more likely to succeed when we find a cadre of friends and supporters to help us push for improvement together.

Finally, if you'd like me to help your organization, send me an email to set up a free thirty-minute conversation: Will.Thalheimer@Work-Learning.com.

# EPILOGUE

## AUDACITY FOR THE FUTURE OF THE WORKPLACE LEARNING FIELD

THIS BOOK HAS ENDED, BUT IT IS PART of a larger vision. After working in the workplace learning-and-performance field for almost thirty years, I—and a number of people with whom I commiserate—have concluded that our field is underprofessionalized and is thus producing an abundance of mediocre results.

Within the span of my career, research psychologists have been able to confirm and illuminate key factors that are critical to any type of learning intervention. Similarly, research on training has demonstrated that additional supports are crucial in creating success. We now know a great deal about what needs to be done—but the large majority of us are still not creating effective learning interventions.

Curiosity has made me wonder why we aren't doing what needs to be done. What are the forces that sustain our mediocrity? Poor smile-sheet design is a potent factor, but it is only one of many such factors.

### We Need to Work Together!

My thinking is this: For our field to become professionalized at a higher level, we need to attack each of the factors that prod our mediocrity with the full force of research-based practical wisdom. This book is a first step, but it is only a small step in a journey I hope to walk with others. I know my audacity here will be a turnoff to some, and I know that I'll likely generate critics and lose business because I'm putting my audacity into the public view—but I'm doing this intentionally to gain the help of folks who are willing to stand up for better learning practices. We need to politely, respectfully, and energetically move the field to a new plane of professionalism.

The truth is that we have in our field an undersized but dedicated cadre of brilliant, passionate, and tireless champions of good learning-and-performance approaches. If you are one of this band of outliers, let us join together in moving the field forward. If you are not yet one, find people doing great work and learn from them.

My plan is to share what I have learned in a series of books over the next few years. These books will be designed specifically to attack the fundamental forces that are pushing us backward. If you'd like to stay in touch and join me on this journey, sign up for my email list at www.work-learning.com/sign-up.html.

### How You Can Help Me Spread the Word

If you liked this book, pass it along to your colleagues, blog about it, tweet about it, write an honest review of it, or rate it on Amazon.com (or other book websites). Better yet, buy several copies and gift them to friends and colleagues.

Send folks to www.SmileSheets.com. When you buy the book directly from me at SmileSheets.com, I get a much, much, much higher percentage of the revenues than if you buy it elsewhere! It's only a slight exaggeration to say that in buying my book you can pay to support my writing and research—or you can give your money to the online booksellers.

Consider hiring me to help your organization. Translating scientific research rarely pays even a penny. Compensation comes when the research is shared in keynotes, workshops, learning audits, learning evaluations, and consulting. Let me share my knowledge with you and your organization. Contact me at Will.Thalheimer@Work-Learning.com.

Thank you for supporting my work! Thank you for creating great learning! Thank you for helping the learning field!

Will Thalheimer

# REFERENCES

Alliger, G. M., Tannenbaum, S. I., Bennett, W., Jr., Traver, H., & Shotland, A. (1997). A meta-analysis of the relations among training criteria. *Personnel Psychology, 50*, 341–358.

Bahrick, H. P., & Hall, L. K. (2005). The importance of retrieval failures to long-term retention: A metacognitive explanation of the spacing effect. *Journal of Memory and Language, 52*, 566–577.

Bjork, R. A., & Richardson-Klavehn, A. (1989). On the puzzling relationship between environmental context and human memory. In C. Izawa (Ed.) *Current Issues in Cognitive Processes: The Tulane Floweree Symposium on Cognition,* pp. 313–344. Hillsdale, NJ: Erlbaum.

Boehle, S. (2006). Are you too nice to train? *Training Magazine*, August.

Bransford, J. D., Franks, J. J., Morris, C. D., & Stein, B. S. (1979). Some general constraints on learning and memory research. In L. S. Cermak & F. I. M. Craik (Eds.), *Levels of Processing in Human Memory*, pp. 331–354. Hillsdale, NJ: Erlbaum.

Brown, P. C., Roediger, H. L., III, & McDaniel, M. A. (2014). *Make It Stick: The Science of Successful Learning*. Cambridge, MA: Belknap Press of Harvard University Press.

Cain, L. F., & Willey, R. (1939). The effect of spaced learning on the curve of retention. *Journal of Experimental Psychology, 25*, 209–214.

Carpenter, S. K., Cepeda, N. J., Rohrer, D., Kang, S. H. K., & Pashler, H. (2012). Using spacing to enhance diverse forms of learning: Review of recent research and implications for instruction. *Educational Psychology Review, 24* (3), 369–378.

Crowder, R. G. (1976). *Principles of Learning and Memory*. Hillsdale, NJ: Erlbaum.

Davies, G. (1986). Context effects in episodic memory: A review. *Cahiers de Psychologie Cognitive, 6*, 157–174.

Delaney, P. F., Verkoeijen, P. P. J. L., & Spirgel, A. (2010). Spacing and testing effects: A deeply critical, lengthy, and at times discursive review of the literature. In B. H. Ross (Ed.), *The Psychology of Learning and Motivation.* Vol. 53, *Advances in Research and Theory,* pp. 63–147. San Diego: Elsevier Academic Press.

Dempster, F. N. (1988). The spacing effect: A case study in the failure to apply the results of psychological research. *American Psychologist, 43*, 627–634.

Dempster, F. N. (1989). Spacing effects and their implications for theory and practice. *Educational Psychology Review, 1*, 309–330.

Dempster, F. N. (1996). Distributing and managing the conditions of encoding and practice. In E. L. Bjork & R. A. Bjork (Eds.), *Memory,* pp. 317–344. San Diego: Academic Press.

Donovan, J. J., & Radosevich, D. J. (1999). A meta-analytic review of the distribution of practice effect: Now you see it, now you don't. *Journal of Applied Psychology, 84,* 795–805.

Eich, J. E. (1980). The cue dependent nature of state dependent retrieval. *Memory and Cognition, 8*, 157–173.

Fiske, S. T., Cuddy, A. J. C., & Glick, P. (2007). Universal dimensions of social cognition: Warmth and competence. *Trends in Cognitive Sciences, 11*(2), 77–83.

Glenberg, A. M. (1979). Component-levels theory of the effects of spacing and repetitions on recall and recognition. *Memory & Cognition, 7*, 95–112.

Gollwitzer, P. M., & Sheeran, P. (2006). Implementation intentions and goal achievement: A meta-analysis of effects and processes. *Advances in Experimental Social Psychology, 38*, 69–119.

Hintzman, D. L. (1974). Theoretical implications of the spacing effect. In R. L. Solso (Ed.), *Theories in Cognitive Psychology: The Loyola Symposium,* pp. 77–99. Potomac, MD: Erlbaum.

Kirschner, P. A., & van Merriënboer, J. J. G. (2013). Do learners really know best? Urban legends in education. *Educational Psychologist, 48*(3), 169–183.

Lee, T. D., & Genovese, E. D. (1988). Distribution of practice in motor skill acquisition: Different effects for discrete and continuous tasks. *Research Quarterly for Exercise and Sport, 60*, 59–65.

Melton, A. W. (1970). The situation with respect to the spacing of repetitions and memory. *Journal of Verbal Learning and Verbal Behavior, 9*, 596–606.

Rea, C. P., & Modigliani, V. (1988). Educational implications of the spacing effect. In M. M. Gruneberg, P. E. Morris, & R. N. Sykes (Eds.) *Practical Aspects of Memory: Current Research and Issues.* Vol. 1, *Memory in Everyday Life,* pp. 402–406. New York: John Wiley & Sons.

Roediger, H. L., III, & Guynn, M. J. (1996). Retrieval processes. In E. L. Bjork & R. A. Bjork (Eds.), *Memory,* pp. 197–236. San Diego: Academic Press.

Ruch, T. C. (1928). Factors influencing the relative economy of massed and distributed practice in learning. *Psychological Review, 35*, 19–45.

Salas, E., Tannenbaum, S. I., Kraiger, K., & Smith-Jentsch, K. A. (2012). The science of training and development in organizations: What matters in practice. *Psychological Science in the Public Interest, 13*(2), 74–101.

Shrock, S. A., & Coscarelli, W. C. (2007). *Criterion-Referenced Test Development: Technical and Legal Guidelines for Corporate Training,* 3rd ed. San Francisco: Wiley.

Sitzmann, T., Brown, K. G., Casper, W. J., Ely, K., & Zimmerman, R. D. (2008). A review and meta-analysis of the nomological network of trainee reactions. *Journal of Applied Psychology, 93*(2), 280–295.

Smith, S. M. (1988). Environmental context-dependent memory. In G. M. Davies & D. M. Thomson (Eds.), *Memory in Context: Context in Memory,* pp. 13–34. Chichester, UK: Wiley.

Smith, S. M., & Vela, E. (2001). Environmental context-dependent memory: A review and meta-analysis. *Psychonomic Bulletin & Review, 8*, 203–220.

Tulving, E., & Thompson, D. M. (1973). Encoding specificity and retrieval processes in episodic memory. *Psychological Review, 80*, 352–373.

# INDEX

# ABOUT THE AUTHOR

Will Thalheimer is a learning expert, researcher, instructional designer, speaker, and writer. He holds an MBA from Drexel University and a PhD in Educational Psychology: Human Learning and Cognition from Columbia University. He has worked in the learning-and-performance field since 1985, playing a diverse set of roles including leadership trainer, instructional designer, simulation architect, project manager, business product line manager, researcher, and consultant.

Beginning in 1998, Dr. Thalheimer dedicated his career to bridging the gap between research and practice in the workplace learning field, founding Work-Learning Research, Inc., as his research and consulting practice.

His clients have included giant multinationals, elearning companies, government agencies, trade associations, and institutions of higher learning.

In 2007 Dr. Thalheimer published a seminal research-to-practice report titled *Measuring Learning Results: Creating Fair and Valid Assessments by Considering Findings from Fundamental Learning Research*. Since then he has been asked to lead workshops, write articles, do research, and give keynote addresses on the topic of learning measurement.